MORE ADVANCE PRAISE FOR ...

Technology Paradise Lost

Dispensing with the idea that the market will go back to normal, Keller argues persuasively that we're seeing a permanent, structural change. One of the best business-oriented information management books I've read.

—DAVID F. CARR
SENIOR TECHNOLOGY ANALYST, *BASELINE*

an extremely accurate picture of IT history and its implications on future IT spending ... provides a wealth of information and tips for both buyers and sellers, and makes informed predictions the investment community should value as well.

—CARL DILL, FORMER CIO
OF AOL/TIME-WARNER

Keller puts his finger on what really changed in the information technology market. Read this book and discover why information technology is finally poised to deliver on the promises of decades past.

—SANJAY KUMAR, CEO
COMPUTER ASSOCIATES

confronts the lack of financial discipline and accountability in IT with hard-hitting analysis *and* pragmatic strategies

—BRYAN STOLLE
CEO AND CHAIRMAN OF THE BOARD
AGILE SOFTWARE CORP.

Keller does a creditable job on the exuberance in technology buying of the late 90s, and provides a pragmatic checklist for the new market realities.

—JEREMY COOTE
PRESIDENT, MANUGISTICS

Technology Paradise Lost

*Why Companies
Will Spend Less
to Get More from
Information Technology*

ERIK KELLER

MANNING

Greenwich
(74° w. long.)

For online information and ordering of this and other Manning
books, go to www.manning.com. The publisher offers discounts
on this book when ordered in quantity. For more information,
please contact:

Special Sales Department
Manning Publications Co.
209 Bruce Park Avenue   Fax: (203) 661-9018
Greenwich, CT 06830   email: orders@manning.com

HD
30.2
. K4553
2004

♾ Recognizing the importance of preserving what has been written, it is
Manning's policy to have the books we publish printed on acid-free
paper, and we exert our best efforts to that end.

Library of Congress Cataloging-in-Publication Data
Keller, Erik, 1957-
    Technology paradise lost: why companies will spend less to
    get more from information technology / Erik Keller.— 1st ed.
       p.   cm.
    Includes bibliographical references and index.
    ISBN 1-932394-13-3
    1. Information technology--Finance. I. Title.
HD30.2.K4553   2004
004'.068'1—dc22   2004001865
                            CIP

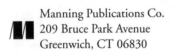

Manning Publications Co.   Copyeditor: Tiffany Taylor
209 Bruce Park Avenue   Typesetter: Dottie Marsico
Greenwich, CT 06830   Cover designer: Leslie Haimes

Cover illustration, courtesy of Dover Publications, Inc., New York.
From Gustave Dore's Illustrations for *Paradise Lost*

Printed in the United States of America
1 2 3 4 5 6 7 8 9 10 – CR – 08 07 06 05 04

To my father, Ralph James,
who taught me how to think, and

To my mother, Norma Jean, and my wife, Juana Maria,
who showed me how to love

contents

preface

Evaluating big IT projects and trends has consumed a large part of my professional life. After graduating from engineering school in 1979, I spent nearly a decade as a technical journalist, reporting on technologies ranging from robots that painted automobiles, to voice-recognition systems that took orders over the phone, to software that controlled and managed the brewing of beer. I toured hundreds of facilities in the United States and learned firsthand how companies used technology. When the technology was used well, the results were amazing. There was always a risk of failure, however, when companies jumped into a technology too quickly.

I then became a technology analyst and spent over a decade at Gartner Inc., starting when it was shy of $40 million per year in revenues and leaving when revenues had grown above $600 million. During that time, I became a trusted advisor to both sellers and buyers of complex technologies, particularly in the area of back-office and operations software. I worked with many of the Fortune 500 companies around the world as well as some of the largest software providers, including SAP, Oracle, Computer Associates, and IBM. During my tenure at Gartner, I advised more than 1,000 companies.

As I spent more time with buyers I began to see that the promise of technology was not always fulfilled. Even when projects were

successful in the beginning, they were often followed by unantici-
pated difficulties downstream.

"How do you do a live upgrade with R/3 [SAP's ERP system]?"
asked a client over lunch one day. I didn't have the faintest idea—
R/3 infrastructure was covered by another Gartner analyst. He continued: "If we do it the way that SAP recommends, we will have to
shut down our systems for four days. I don't know how we'd do it."
I still remember my sharp sense of embarrassment. Here was a technology that I had readily recommended to the company, yet I had
no idea of some of the consequences of its use. I passed the buck to
my Gartner colleague.

Another time, I was working with a client who wanted to replace
a perfectly good piece of software with a new one because the older
one ran on mainframe technology. I kept trying to talk him out of
it, encouraging him to look for alternatives. I couldn't understand
what the point was. The client made it very clear to me: "It's a good
career move for me."

By the end of my tenure at Gartner, in the late 1990s, I was
spending more time helping clients clean up problems than launch
new technology initiatives. By then I had serious doubts about the
widely held theory that technology would always help businesses
better themselves.

In the next stretch of my career, as a consultant, I started to look
with fresh eyes at what it takes to be successful with technology.
Over the next few years, I found more questions than answers.

Back in the 1990s, it appeared that an irrational exuberance for
IT-based capital spending grabbed hold of corporate America—and
didn't let go for a long time. (Ironically, Europe and Asia did not
catch this illness to the same degree, though I had non-U.S. clients
who made mistakes similar to those of their U.S. counterparts.)

When the exuberance finally died down in 2001, corporate technology buying was left in a state of exhaustion and malaise, with little future direction. A new way of thinking and implementing IT
was long overdue.

In 2002, the Sand Hill Group asked me to discuss the future
of the software industry during its annual Enterprise conference.
This was well past the bursting of the IT stock-market bubble, yet

few pundits or companies believed that the worst was over. My presentation, "The New Competition," told how new technology combined with a new buying sobriety and economic shortfalls had changed the landscape of corporate IT buying and selling, perhaps forever. While it was a downbeat presentation to more than 200 CEOs and decision makers in the IT industry, it was received thoughtfully.

Before dinner, one conference attendee approached me and asked, "If things are going to become so bad, how will you make a living?" We both laughed, and although he may have been kidding, I felt a twinge of discomfort. A change was in the air for corporate buyers and sellers of technology, but I couldn't put my finger on what it was. Unlike during the previous 15 years, there was no Big Thing. No Y2K. No ERP. No Internet mania to stoke the hype fires. Instead, many small things were happening: major companies were experimenting with offshore development; clients were choosing to build open-source software solutions for under $100,000 rather than buying $2 million software packages; CIOs were looking to cut back rather than accelerate spending. Everyone was waiting for the Next Big Thing—but what was it?

The answer may seem obvious given all the technological advances in cell phones, broadband Internet access, DVDs, instant messaging, and personal computers. But we need to distinguish between *consumer* technologies, which are booming, and *corporate* technologies, which are not.

I was not the only one thinking this way. In mid-2003, Nicholas Carr's eight-page article "IT Doesn't Matter" in the *Harvard Business Review* triggered a firestorm of criticism. Regardless of the details of Carr's argument that the strategic importance of technology had diminished, his article served a useful purpose in triggering serious public debate. This debate covers three important themes: 1) the appropriate role of IT within business, 2) the right level of investment in technology, and 3) the benefits ultimately derived from technology.

With this book, I am attempting to consider all sides. You will find discussions and examples identifying participants with no more than a first name (to protect the confidentiality of my clients, it was not possible to identify them more precisely). All of the examples and conversations described in the book are real; they took place at various points over the course of my career.

In contrast to much of the research done by traditional analyst firms (which assumes and, in fact, promotes more spending in IT), this book maintains that companies can move ahead over the next few years *without* large increases in their IT budgets. The only thing a company needs is a different perspective.

A lot of books and reports focusing on business improvement via technology have a catch: Before you can hope to see any benefits, you are required to spend *more* money on a new technology than what you initially paid. While I have favorite technologies that I believe can improve business processes, those technologies are not the subject of this book. This book is about increasing the effectiveness of technology while reducing IT expenses. Instead of a silver-bullet technology, companies need silver-haired thinking, grounded in solid returns, not airy promises.

Let me be blunt: The 1990s way of doing business is dead. Buyers and sellers of technology have two choices: Deny the practice of spending less and getting more, and be rolled over by change—or embrace the change and move forward into a new business environment.

If I am right and we are living through an IT inflection point, it is useful to know that such points occurred in all major technological revolutions dating back to the industrial revolution of the 18th century. Carlota Perez's excellent book, *Technological Revolutions and Financial Capital*, places IT as the fifth such revolution. Nothing is new about this revolution except that few people remember the prior ones.

These inflection points have one consistent feature: The companies that recognize the nature of change before everyone else prosper greatly. The goal of this book is to help anyone whose livelihood depends on the IT industry to navigate the difficult times ahead.

acknowledgments

Having the name of a single author, or even a few, on a book such as this is an injustice, because so many people have contributed to its genesis as well as its morphing through the research and writing process. To all of you, I am grateful for the generosity of your time and input. Many people and companies contributed to this book, but in particular I would like to thank the following:

All my clients, former and present, for letting me become a part of their decision teams. The insights I have received from you are core to the premise of this book.

The many companies that permitted me to profile their use of technology. Their views and honesty provided a framework for many of the chapters. In particular, I'd like to thank Marvin Balliet of Merrill Lynch; John Boushy and Gary Loveman of Harrah's; Tom Claydon of JetBlue; and Toby Redshaw of Motorola. Not to be overlooked are the many other individuals and companies who may be anonymous in the book but who have earned my deepest appreciation.

The companies that are helping users to better understand and manage their IT costs in a new and innovative way. Many are embarking on this journey, and a few have shared their visions and successes with me. Thanks to BDNA, Descartes Systems Group, JetStream Group, Salesforce.com, Symphony Technology Group, Tata

Consultancy Services, VMware, Veritas, and others who gave me insights to how buyers can spend less and get more from their technology investments.

All of my reviewers, who kept me honest and focused. As a group they were invaluable to shaping and giving this book life. They include Dave Caruso, Kevin Brooks, Isaac Cheifetz, John Crabtree, Nathan Egge, Lee Harding, Sabrina Horn, Gregory S. Hopper, Randolph S. Kahle, John D. Mitchell, David Paine, Patrick Peak, Eric Stahl, and Vic Zonko.

Former colleagues, who let me pester them for advice and guidance in various areas where their expertise enabled me to better explore and understand the nuances that this book examines. They include Dave Burdick, Andrew Dailey, Ken McGee, Bill McNee, Igor Stenmark, George Weiss, and Mary Welch. Special thanks go to Chris Jones, who helped to rid the manuscript of sloppy ideas and indulgent writing. He was key to the creation of Buyers' and Sellers' survival guides. Also, many thanks to Vinnie Mirchandani, who patiently helped me understand the benefits and challenges of offshoring as well as the potential for savings in IT contracts. Also, my gratitude goes to Donna Fluss, who introduced me to my publisher and watered the seed that led to this book.

The organizations and research companies that were so generous in letting me reproduce their graphics and information, including Alinean, AMR Research, BDNA, Gartner Inc., Mc Kinsey and Co., NASSCOM, Saugatuck Technology, Strassmann Inc, the University of Cambridge, and the University of Colorado. Special thanks to M.R. Rangaswami of the Sand Hill Group, who gave me access to companies and ideas that proved essential to the book.

Members of the Manning Publications team, who were helpful and patient in getting me through the book process. Special thanks to my publisher, Marjan Bace, whose guidance and vision helped make this book a reality.

My wife, Juana Maria, whose patience, advice, and love were essential to getting the best out of me. By reading the manuscript and providing wise counsel, she kept me on track. Without her, there would be no book.

Finally, *all the companies—buyers and sellers—that seek the best from technology by following the vision of spending less to get more.*

Even after all of this wonderful help, mistakes will appear in the book. They are all mine. Mea culpa.

CHAPTER ONE

PARADISE LOST?

MASSIVE CHANGE OCCURS QUIETLY, insidiously, and without apparent direction. A single event didn't cause the collapse of the Antarctic Larsen B Ice Shelf; instead, the accumulation of countless tiny changes—a slight rise in temperature, the appearance of a few fissures, small streams forming on the surface of the glacier, deep cracks and chasms opening at an accelerated rate—together and applied over time had catastrophic results, as recorded by satellite photos in early 2002.[1] In a little over five weeks, a mass of ice approximately the size of Rhode Island (weighing 720 billion tons and approximately 220 meters thick) broke apart, shattered, and separated, as shown in the figure on the next page.

About the same time, the information technology (IT) business was beginning to experience a similar accumulation of unremarkable changes set into motion by a deteriorating global economy. The signs were there: missed revenue targets, corporate layoffs, and an overall industry malaise, all of which were expected to stop by the end of 2003. These initial changes in the industry were widely dismissed as cyclical.

The collapse of the Larsen B Ice Shelf. Between January 31, 2002 (left) and March 5, 2002 (right), the Larsen B Ice Shelf in Antarctica broke apart due to the global increase in temperature and other factors. No one foresaw this catastrophic event even though the forces that caused it had been occurring for many years. *Source: MODIS images courtesy of NASA's Terra satellite, supplied by Ted Scambos, National Snow and Ice Data Center, University of Colorado, Boulder.*

The consensus is that once the economy rebounds, IT spending and growth will continue to climb as they have for the last 20 years. However, this is a dangerous and illogical assumption that time will prove wrong. In fact, both business and technology trends predict that IT spending will decline, while delivering higher levels of business value and productivity. The buying and selling of IT is about to change forever. Consider the following:

- A software programmer in India making $5,000 a year putting the finishing touches on a new procurement program for a Midwest manufacturer
- Technology budgets that consume more than 50 percent of capital goods spending being increasingly scrutinized
- Multimillion-dollar software investments being abandoned for approaches costing a tenth as much
- IT budgets being slashed without a discernible difference in service or productivity
- Technology product companies giving away software products while increasing their service revenue
- Free, open source software delivering the same value as high-priced systems

Not unlike the opening scenes of a suspense film, these individual events appear to have little connection. Taken together, though, they are clues to understanding an underlying change in the IT industry, in much the same way that unseen forces such as global warming caused the Larsen B Ice Shelf to collapse.

A NEW ORDER EMERGES

We take many things for granted today that would not be possible without the sophisticated and well-deployed technology base that exists. Applications ranging from using credit cards at gas pumps, to buying products over the Internet, to running power plants, to tracking packages sent around the world, are essential to companies and consumers. Such applications will never go away—and they shouldn't. However, there has been a high cost for some of these conveniences.

For years, corporate use of IT has been plagued with overcomplexity, redundancy, and wastefulness. That is about to change. Companies like Harrah's, JetBlue, Motorola, and Merrill Lynch (see chapters 8 and 9 for examples) are starting to realize that they can do much more with much less. These lessons, along with some new technology approaches, outsourcing opportunities, and a focus on IT spending, will allow corporations to increase their use of IT at a lower initial and ongoing cost.

IT buyers and sellers will see a dramatic change in the way they do business. IT sellers will need to meet the new corporate IT buying requirements to survive in the economically competitive environment. IT buyers must also change the way they deploy and justify their technology purchases. Much more business savvy will be needed from both groups for the following reasons:

- **Technologists must deliver business value.** The view that IT must be controlled by IT purists is just plain wrong. Business sectors that take control of and understand all aspects of their IT budgets are positioned to profit. Sellers will no longer be able to dazzle buyers with the promise of hot technology. Return on investment (ROI) and business understanding will be required. (See chapters 4 and 8 for more on ROI and IT budgets.)

- **Cheaper and simpler is better.** Complicated technology deployments and architectures deliver less benefit to companies than systems that accomplish things more quickly and cheaply. Easy-to-use and 80 percent solutions are providing better business benefits at lower costs than complex customized technologies. (Chapter 6 discusses these types of strategies.)

- **Companies have underutilized technology.** A vast array of IT assets go underutilized within corporate walls. This realization is forcing many companies to use what they have or throw it out. The rebalancing and rationalization of IT asset portfolios are allowing companies to spend much less on IT, as you'll see in chapter 5.

- **Labor costs are going down.** IT support and labor are shifting to India and other low-cost nations. Employees and consultants must either deliver higher value to customers/employers or accept lower compensation. Companies can trim a large part of their tactical technology labor spending by outsourcing as much as 70 percent of their IT labor. (See chapter 7 for a discussion of offshoring.)

- **New buying and selling models are emerging.** Buyers are shying away from investing millions of dollars up front for projects that require years to realize business benefits. Sellers are no longer able to afford year-long selling cycles that consume many people and dollars. Chapters 10 and 11 will show you how to take advantage of these new buying and selling models.

The days of "caviar" spending are gone and are being replaced with a new "pork and beans" attitude.

New software attitude

Moore's Law, formulated by Intel founder Gordon Moore in 1965, predicts a doubling of the integrated circuit price/performance ratio every 18 to 24 months.[2] Hardware has followed this route, but software has not. Standardized technologies and a better understanding of how software should best be deployed have emerged. The development of open source products, including the operating system Linux and other "freeware" initiatives, has changed the market, forcing prices down in many sectors in a "Moore-like" fashion. Other factors, such as Extensible Markup Language (XML) and web services as well as new approaches in architecture, are changing the software cost equation for companies. (Again, check out chapter 6 for more on this topic.)

These developments have led companies to find and deploy cost-effective alternative solutions that are driving down IT software spending. They include the use of open source software, the expansion of Microsoft into corporate computing, and cheaper and easier connectivity via Internet protocols and specifications. These solutions are decreasing the cost and complexity of integrating different systems within corporations.

New labor attitude

As software prices drop, so does the cost of labor needed to install and maintain the software. Offshoring is reducing costs for sellers and buyers at an accelerating pace, as you'll see in chapter 7. Countries such as India, Russia, and other developing nations have a labor-cost advantage of up to 15-to-1 over the United States and Western Europe. A booming infrastructure and an employee pool offering a 40- to 70-percent reduction in personnel costs for programming are being tapped. As a result, a few U.S. companies have already sent more than 20,000 technical jobs to India and other low-cost countries.

Along with this trend is the offshoring of entire business processes. U.S. companies might have underestimated both the quality and capacity of offshoring companies; for example, some global firms based in India have capabilities exceeding their large U.S. counterparts.

Together these trends will have a large impact on IT deployments and budgets in years to come.

New buyer attitude

Given the availability of low-priced software and cheap labor, a great potential exists to decrease IT spending while holding the line on service levels and capabilities. It's not likely that the free and easy spending of IT in years past will ever come back to corporations.

After years of questionable returns, cost overruns, and increased complexity, companies are pushing financial rigor to IT groups. Here are some of the approaches:

- Managing and rationalizing IT asset bases; eliminating redundant, unnecessary systems along with their associated maintenance costs
- Showing "tough love" to suppliers and internal champions of technology
- Adopting a "show-me" attitude
- Putting business units in charge of technology budgets and forcing technologists to justify all technology investments, even "pure" ones

Chapters 5, 9, and 10 will examine how companies are reevaluating their IT investment plans and are getting much more from technology while spending much less.

New seller attitude

All of these buyer changes will make the flush days of IT spending a thing of the past. In fact, many of the corporate IT markets may soon resemble the rough-and-tough consumer electronics market with ruthless price-cutting and even tighter margins. This type of environment will extend to employees of both buyers and sellers as the new economics of corporate IT puts tight wage pressures on all workers. Opportunities for future growth will still exist, but in a very different way than in the past. Some significant changes we can expect are:

- New selling and buying models that will be deployed to accommodate slower and more cautious buying patterns. Subscription and on-demand-type selling will become more commonplace. To accommodate these new selling models, sellers will need to slash their cost models by at least 20 percent.
- Many of the traditional technical career paths in IT will disappear. Best opportunities will exist for those whose understanding of the business complements their technical skills. Expertise in either an individual industry (e.g., automotive,

financial services) or a function (e.g., logistics, marketing) will be essential.

Only those technology sellers with a tight market focus, realistic growth expectations, and tight cost controls will succeed. Rather than attempt to become the next mega-vendor, a company might need to focus on a strategy that will help it become a desirable acquisition target. Chapter 11 will examine how the changes in buying will affect IT employees and sellers.

WHY NOW?

Like the factors leading up to the collapse of the Larsen B Ice Shelf, problems with corporate IT use have been insidious and have been accumulating for some time. In 2000, headlines started to hit the *Wall Street Journal* and *Fortune Magazine*. Beyond the collapse of Internet dot.com companies and technologies, there were stories of large corporate failures driven by IT. One such example was how a bungled $100-million-plus enterprise resource planning/supply chain management (ERP/SCM) integration at Hershey's crippled the company, as well as analyst reports revealing how both company and industry initiatives had failed. (See chapters 3 and 4 for more examples.)

Back in the mid-1990s, Gartner Inc. (my employer at the time and a leading IT research company based in Stamford, CT) well knew that such problems existed but did not publicize them outside the client base. I remember a conversation with a European client that revolved around a $50 million implementation of SAP's general-ledger functionality.[3]

"It was our fault as much as SAP's," the client said. "Its software was complex, and we just threw consultants at the problem. Some days we were burning $50,000 in fees just to have people sit around and wait for our decision. We learned a lot but at a huge cost."

Such stories were not common just to SAP. Bad buying and implementation practices as well as unclear returns are just two of the many reasons technology spending growth will not return to its glory days. With this new focus and operational discipline, the review and justification of IT for corporations will most likely become similar to that required for any new piece of capital equipment. This trend was first manifested in 2002 when many chief information officers (CIOs) were given incentives to spend less than their budget called for and nearly 60 percent complied, according to a Morgan Stanley survey of CIOs.[4] One of my neighbors, the chief financial officer (CFO) for a multinational consumer goods company, summed up this point nicely while raking leaves one day.

"IT has driven many of the initiatives in our company, many of which were viewed as failures with little return," he said. "The trouble is that they are rarely aligned with the problems we are having, which can range from the price of transportation to the price of a raw material. We used to ask for a capital return of 10 percent before we would approve something; now we ask for 30 [percent] and also which workers or machines will be replaced. If they need a requisition of $150,000, I need to see $150,000 of people or equipment go in short order."

This ruthless type of quantification is not something IT buyers or sellers are accustomed to. In fact, such proof is hard to find when searching through most technology vendors' web sites or marketing literature. Their value proposition has always been based on faith rather than cold, hard economic arguments. This is a reality that they must align themselves with, because an increased percentage of buying oversight is coming from CFOs and business unit leaders.

A recent survey by *CFO Magazine* indicated that CFOs are taking a much larger role in spending approval and corporate governance.[5] Such professionals care little for the bells and whistles of the latest Intel chip or new web service, but instead want to know how the new technology will cut costs or increase revenues or profitability. As the figure on the next page illustrates, IT sellers will need to deliver highly tangible benefits that can be translated to profits or losses and communicate these benefits in simple terms.

The equation is simple: The amount of money companies spend on IT will be measured against the business benefits received. This investment includes expenses of people, products, and services. The benefits range from quantifiable productivity benefits, such as reducing the cost of labor, to qualifiable ones, such as a better

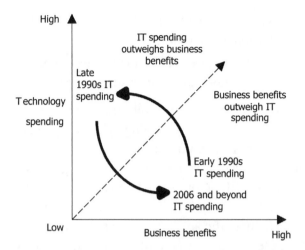

Business benefits compared with technology expenditures. In the 1990s, companies spent more on their technology investments than they received in business benefits. This tide of spending is about to turn back as companies focus more on quantifying the business benefits received from their IT spending.

customer experience on the corporate web site. Such benefits will be difficult for traditional buyers of technology to deliver, given the systems that must be supported and the legacy of investments.

A MESSY LEGACY

IT is often discussed as something new and exciting, but it is a tough and often inflexible environment. This environment was created over the last 30 years by the fire drill–like atmosphere of daily IT operations combined with inconsistent strategic initiatives. More to the point, IT buyers spend approximately 70 percent of their total budgets on *existing* systems.[6] There are a few simple reasons for this high level of spending:

- Additional annual payments of up to 28 percent of the initial list price for installed and supported software solutions
- Upgrades of desktop hardware and software in cycles of three year or fewer
- Consultants charging between $100 and $300 per hour for services

- Enterprise software upgrades costing anywhere from 20 to 100 percent of the initial implementation cost
- Integration between existing systems, altering business practices, and expensive reimplementation of existing systems

These actions have lured corporations into collecting myriad technologies that are incompatible and ever changing. They range from COBOL-based custom programs running on IBM mainframe technology that process insurance claims to Java applets running on PCs that check the location and tracking of ordered goods. Nearly every major corporation has such a collection of systems whose contents have increased dramatically over the last decade. Many of these new options substantially increase the amount of money a company spends on IT without a corresponding business benefit.

Companies are now deciding whether their investments will remain a La Brea tar pit of economic debt and corporate waste or become a renewed set of assets positioned to deliver corporate benefits. Unlike in the past, many new options, mechanisms, and techniques now exist to help companies work their way out of their respective tar pits and become more agile in their use of technology.

A METAPHOR FOR SURVIVAL

Sir Ernest Shackleton made a journey from England to Antarctica in August 1914. With a crew of 27 men, he sailed into dangerous waters on the *Endurance,* became trapped in ice (as shown in the photographs on the next page), and ultimately watched as his ship was consumed by the harsh Antarctic environment. His initial mission to explore was quickly replaced with another: how to get himself and all his men home safely. Amazingly, he did, delivering all of them back to safety in September 1916.

His passion for life and singular drive for survival are what brought him and his men home safely. Shackleton's choices were more critical than those that IT buyers and sellers will face in the coming years but were perhaps no less challenging, strategically.

Businesses will continue investing in IT, but the growth experienced in the past 15 years, particularly in software and services, will not continue. This is in sharp contrast to the accepted opinion of

Endurance **trapped in (left) and then consumed by (right) an ice pack near Antarctica in 1915. The story of Sir Ernest Shackleton is one about leadership and survival, and it serves as an inspiration to anyone facing insurmountable obstacles.** *Source: Licensed with permission of the Scott Polar Research Institute, University of Cambridge.*

many industry pundits, research firms, investors, and companies who believe that once the world economy turns around, the type of growth experienced in the past will continue. Even the relatively modest (by historical standards) growth estimates of double the Gross Domestic Product (GDP) put forth by seasoned companies such as IBM are a stretch.[7]

Indeed, it appears that peak corporate technology expenditures in the United States approaching $1 trillion yearly are poised to enter the slow-growing, mature phase of their lifecycle. In fact, they could drop significantly in the next few years if companies become seriously focused on reducing waste and obtaining more benefits from IT expenditures. On the other hand, because necessity is the mother of invention, an era of scarcity could also trigger tremendous innovation in how existing technologies are used.

THE IMPACT OF CHANGE

All of this points to one conclusion: "The Next New Thing" in IT is not a "thing" at all, but a new way of thinking—an evolutionary leap forward in which the needs of humankind, money, and machine are blended together in harmony.

The "technology-thing" of the past is quickly being replaced by the "business-thing" as defined by those who master spreadsheets and ledgers. It's the bottom line that survives this battle. A quiet pragmatism will emerge within a handful of hardy companies, one that will call for a simpler, more efficient, business-driven view of how to deploy technology.

The new business-thing is a bitter pill to swallow for sellers and buyers with a vested interest in the production and purchase of more technology. However, it is proving to be therapeutic for corporations that are seeing an increase in IT effectiveness and a decrease in IT spending through the exploitation of new technologies along with buying and management approaches. Those in denial about such a conclusion will be sorely affected by these changes.

IT is not immune to the same business forces noted by Adam Smith in 1776 in *An Inquiry into the Nature and Causes of the Wealth of Nations*. The "invisible hand" of natural economic law that drove the growth of IT spending in the 1990s can also facilitate its decline. History not only repeats but also follows certain economic laws of "gravity"; what goes up must come down. To understand the future, it is important to examine the trajectory of the past.

CHAPTER TWO

IT SPENDING:
A BRIEF HISTORY

In 1950, there were about 20 automatic calculators and computers in the United States with a total value of around $1 million.
—The Computer Comes of Age[1]

In 2001, corporate information technology spending reached nearly 50 percent of all capitalized goods.
—U.S. Department of Commerce,
Bureau of Economic Analysis[2]

OVER THE PAST 15 YEARS, the IT industry has seen its share of ups and downs, with growth often in the double digits. Much of this growth was due to optimism in the industry itself. For some companies, including Dell, Wal-Mart, and others, this optimism was justified with IT-enabled lower costs and increased revenue. But for most others, it was not.

There was a great deal of trend-buying and a herd mentality for purchasing any new technology that was promoted in *Business Week* or by a prominent market-research company. Appropriations of

$100 million for a new piece of software that met an undefined business need were all too common.

"Why do you need to spend over $100 million on a new ERP system?" I asked Victor (not his real name), the CIO of a major pharmaceutical company. We were having lunch at the 21 Club in New York City.

Victor seemed taken aback by the question. "What do you mean, *why?*" he asked. He was unsure of the business need but was convinced that his company had to install a new ERP system. He had already received a large funding appropriation to start the project. Turning back was not an option, even with potential cost overruns and the possibility of implementation failure. "Let's pick a system." That was his message.

Victor's attitude was not uncommon. "Irrational exuberance" was pervasive throughout the 1990s. Many companies were attempting to deploy technologies costing tens if not hundreds of millions of dollars. Big-bang implementations of complex IT systems were the best game in town for buyers and sellers. But all good (and sometimes bad) things must eventually come to an end.

THE BEGINNING OF A LEGACY

Since the early 1960s, corporate IT spending has steadily accelerated,[3] as the next figure illustrates.

In the early days of computing, a series of slow-to-evolve technological innovations (and associated business benefits) led companies to spend more on technology. The mainframe computers and time-sharing approaches of the 1960s and '70s represented the initial stages of automating back-office functions, such as accounting and payroll, and operational tasks, such as inventory and order management. They were complemented by the distributed computing efforts of the late 1970s and '80s, which helped smaller corporate units or companies to automate similar functions in a more distributed fashion. During this era, minicomputers and PCs supplemented mainframe technology for office-automation tasks like word processing. In 2000, IT spending peaked in total revenue in the United States.

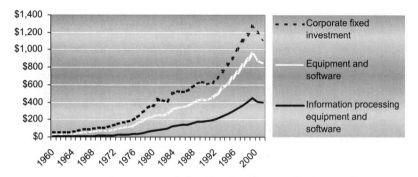

Corporate fixed investment between 1960 and 2002 (in $ billions, actual). Much of the growth of corporate fixed investment in the 1990s was due to IT purchases,[4,5] which have become increasingly important to the U.S. economy. Actual (rather than inflation-indexed) numbers are used in figures throughout this book so that all statistics use the same base. *Source: U.S. Department of Commerce, Bureau of Economic Analysis.*

Before 2001, IT spending had grown for many decades, as you can see in the figure on the next page. A series of new technological milestones kept spending growth up:

- Minicomputers in the 1970s
- The PC in the 1980s
- Client-server technology[6] combined with ERP in the early to mid-1990s
- Y2K fixes in the mid-1990s
- The Internet at the end of the 1990s

Each step represented a different catalyst for increased spending. In the last few years, however, these technology and application platforms have become so competitive that one may completely replace another.

Redundant technologies

The demise of older technologies is often exaggerated. Mainframe computers and COBOL programming were expected to be completely retired by the mid-1990s. That is still far from the truth.

Mainframe computers are still widely used in most corporations today. Major airlines, insurance companies, banks, and other industries use mainframes to run a large array of critical applications.

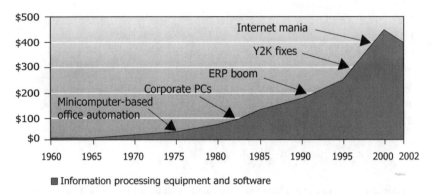

IT capital investment by type between 1960 and 2002 (in $ billions, actual). Over the past 30 years, a set of accelerators has increased the total rate of IT spending. As software spending became dominant in the 1990s, the rates of increase spiked even faster. *Source: BEA and Wapiti LLC.*

In fact, a few years ago, eBay, the online trading company, considered replacing its Unix-based systems with an IBM mainframe because of its business volume and growth. (Sun Microsystems did everything it could to provide the performance and speed eBay needed and was successful in keeping eBay as a customer.)

Most corporations are hesitant to discontinue older business solutions because they still work. As a result, we now find ourselves in an era of redundancy and overlap. Corporations have started to accumulate computer systems the way some farmers accumulate old trucks, tractors, and cars. Each is good for only one or two tasks, but all have to be maintained. As you can see in the previous figure, IT spending increased significantly as a result of numerous factors.

Three legacies from the 1990s

Redundant technologies are not new. In the early 1990s, companies were starting to struggle with overlapping systems in their IT departments. At the time, three types of computer systems were in widespread use:

- Large centralized mainframe computers built by IBM, Hitachi, and others that ran most mission-critical tasks.
- Departmental or minicomputers built by Hewlett-Packard, Digital Equipment Corp., and others that managed inventory at factories and supported office-automation tasks.

- PCs that replaced "dumb terminals" for an increasing number of corporate workers. Personal productivity applications such as word processing and e-mail were used on these systems.

Meanwhile, new client-server systems running the Unix operating system sold by companies such as Sun Microsystems and Hewlett-Packard were becoming a part of corporate computing.

A wide collection of incompatible communication networks was used to connect these devices. Running on these platforms (particularly the mainframe) were custom software packages written in languages such as COBOL, FORTRAN, and PL/1. The fledgling software industry was divided between a few large companies that sold packages for mainframes and many small companies selling packages that ran on minicomputers and PCs.

The first 30 years of IT spending left most corporations with a little of everything. Although many companies tried to narrow these assets as new generations of technology were deployed, most were left with an ever-increasing array of systems.

CHANGE IS HARD

There were several good reasons for the technological redundancy during the 1990s. The new technology could not always handle the business load, the functionality was not totally supported by the newer systems, and it was not always cost effective to roll out a new system worldwide. These realities led to an accumulation of systems (as well as an accumulation of costs) that increased the complexity and budget of information systems in many corporations. The new technology did not always lead to increased productivity, either.

During the 1990s, a Massachusetts Institute of Technology (MIT) professor-turned-high-tech visionary, Dr. Michael Hammer, was extolling business process reengineering (BPR) to corporations. He told companies they needed to dynamically reconfigure their primary business processes—order management and sales support, for example—to better address the needs of their customers. Corporate executives bought into this vision. They hired scores of expensive consultants from the Big Eight accounting firms as well as McKinsey & Company, Boston Consulting Group, and others. But no one, Dr. Hammer included, probed any further to see how these changes would be made or how much they would cost. No software or system existed that would execute Hammer's vision.

As corporations reengineered their business processes, many found that business functions were scattered around their facilities on disparate systems and technologies. Certain core business processes resided on a mainframe in a central location. The newly created BPR-enabled corporation had little use for these old processes, which could not be easily altered. The installed base of technology made it difficult to execute the vision of BPR.

Software is not flexible

The software within large corporations is complex, expensive, and difficult to change. New technologies such as web services, which can simplify application integration and programming, are remedying some of those problems. However, the ability of software to accommodate business-process changes (e.g., a new way to take a customer order) or technological-requirement changes (e.g., updating to a new database version) has historically been overestimated. Such flexibility has always been a holy grail for sellers of software products—and like the search for the grail, it is a quest that has yet to be fulfilled. The reasons for this include:

- The set of business processes captured in software includes many interrelationships that cannot be changed. Even the best programmers can cause system failures by making "trivial" changes.

- Software written for one type of platform (e.g., operating system, database, and others) can rarely be run on another platform without a substantial porting effort. Porting requires that certain aspects of a program be rewritten. A large effort is required to port older applications running on proprietary mainframe and minicomputer operating systems/databases to a new environment; a smaller effort is required for newer systems. For example, many companies have written software for Microsoft's current proprietary environments (Windows and SQL Server) that cannot run on Linux or Unix systems without a complete rewrite.

- Business process flexibility must be initially designed into software. Few packaged applications and even fewer customized solutions written in procedural languages such as COBOL, C, FORTRAN, and others can accommodate changes easily. Newer software development tools have not solved this problem.

- Software documentation for installations and alterations of code is lacking, which inhibits future change.

- A small change in a complex software system can trigger mistakes and failures that cascade throughout multiple programs. Because many corporate applications are integrated in a Gordian Knot of technologies, even the simplest change can be difficult to accomplish.

Suppose that a company that uses a standard cost model in its manufacturing process wants to adopt an activity-based cost model.[7] The software that handles standard costing was not created to handle an activity-based counterpart. A new set of business processes, data linkages, and inputs is required as well as additional integration with such applications as fixed assets and labor-tracking systems. A "simple" business process change requires a major revamping of a software system. Sometimes the changes are so difficult that it is easier and less expensive (from an IT perspective) to purchase and install a new piece of software.

Technical issues that deal with change can be equally daunting. An upgrade to a new version of software (e.g., a database or operating system) can force companies to upgrade many other systems simultaneously that are dependent on those technologies. The recent adoption of web-based applications continues to provide a technical challenge for corporations as few of their legacy applications were designed to accommodate the Web.

Companies quickly decided they needed to implement new systems because of these issues. At the very least, they would have to buy new software. But for many, this change did not lower IT costs. In fact, it accelerated an ever-growing spiral of spending increases.

ENTERPRISE RESOURCE PLANNING

In the early 1990s, enterprise resource planning (ERP), an integrated software suite of financial, human resources, and back-office operational business processes, emerged with the promise of addressing IT and business problems. This new solution required scrapping mainframes; a true ERP system needed to be powered with an open-systems Unix platform.

As with BPR, this vision quickly became reinforced by vendors, consultants, and users. Together they were catalysts to the continuance of IT spending. Buying and recommending these systems became good business. Consultants such as the Big Eight accounting firms and market research firms such as AMR Research, Gartner, META Group, and Forrester Research were caught up in the frenzy of helping companies rip out old systems and install new ones. These companies often walked an ethical tightrope in an effort to do what was best for a company's business and also what they were hired to do. Often they were hired for one simple reason: to reinforce the decision of the client and act as an insurance policy.

"I really like their vision," said Fred, the director of IT for a Midwest manufacturing company of precision-machined parts. "If I have two years to do this, what problems could occur? And [by the way] they promised to migrate me."

Fred was looking to replace a variety of systems with one from Systems Software Associates (SSA), a Chicago-based seller of ERP financial and manufacturing software named BPCS. This company was a dominant seller of software that ran on IBM's AS/400 platform (now called the iSeries). The company had an inspiring but risky plan to move its technology base from this hardware platform and run it on multiple technology platforms, including Unix and Windows NT. No company had successfully pulled off such a move. SSA was telling customers that it could easily migrate them to the new technology without problems. But the company could not demonstrate how well the solution would work in a production setting.

My response to Fred was simple: "A friend of mine told me once that 'Geese migrate, ducks migrate, but software doesn't migrate.'"

I pointed out a variety of risks: a lack of references, a short implementation timeframe, untested technology, unknown software quality, and application performance and costs. Fred would not be dissuaded, however. He had bought into the vision of ERP and wanted me to tell him it was okay to purchase an untested product from SSA.

Eventually, I gave Fred a softened recommendation. I suggested that he wait a few months before starting, provided he had an alternative implementation plan. The client was happy with the recommendation.

Unfortunately, SSA never executed its promising vision, sputtered in the market, filed for bankruptcy protection, and was eventually bought out by Gores Technology Group, which has been reincarnated as SSA Global Technologies. The company has stabilized its product and made a good business of purchasing financially challenged technology companies, including Baan and EXE. Fred's vision was never realized.

Note

In late 2002, two of SSA's executives, Chairman and CEO Roger Covey and former CFO Joseph Skadra, consented to settle a Securities and Exchange Commissions (SEC) suit. "According to the Commission's complaint, Covey and Skadra caused SSA to misstate its financial results during its fiscal years 1994 through 1996 by improperly reporting revenue on sales of a UNIX-language software product before the product was developed sufficiently to support revenue recognition under Generally Accepted Accounting Principles (GAAP). The complaint alleged that Covey and Skadra knew or were reckless in not knowing that the software did not function properly and that there were significant uncertainties about customer acceptance of that software." Covey was fined more than $300,000.[8]

Everyone wins

Fred is just one example of the typical IT director of the 1990s. Few companies were looking at the ramifications of these types of decisions because they proved to be lucrative for everyone. Consultants and analysts increased their clout and their rates. Hardware vendors increased their profits—a new generation of hardware was needed to run ERP software. Software companies—SAP, PeopleSoft, and Oracle[9] in particular—banked large revenues on seven- and eight-figure projects. ERP was also lucrative for a vast array of new infrastructure, telecommunications, and other consulting companies. CIOs and technologists became important corporate figures, managing complex projects that reached hundreds of millions of dollars in size.

Other application software markets added to this base. These included supply chain management (SCM), customer resource management (CRM), and countless other categories. With them came a growing market in systems software to manage and run the complex IT systems that were being created with these applications. Everyone was winning.

A software package that was licensed to a major corporation for $10 million could require an additional $100 million or more for installation. Many companies greatly underestimated the overall cost and complexity of these new projects. Companies were looking for simple answers, but none existed.

The software-to-services ratio

When buying complex technology, companies must look at the total cost of the project, which consists of hardware, software, and services. Because hardware costs have declined greatly, most buyers focus on services and software spending. For most IT projects, internal labor and external services consume the main part of the budget. This variable makes the real cost question: what's the software-to-services ratio for an ERP installation? This is an impossible question to answer without a great deal of understanding about the nature of the project.

I would tell clients, "If you need a number, it can range anywhere from 1.5 to 2 for a very simple installation using plain vanilla [pre-configured] software making few changes to it, with little integration to other systems. On the other hand, big multinational intergalactic implementations requiring lots of customization, integration with legacy systems that change fundamental business processes, can be 10 and above. One client is pushing 20 on a badly run project." From this type of discussion, the client would then be able to estimate the potential range of spending to support a spending request. Sometimes they would request this information in writing.

Enterprise systems became the big game in town during the mid-1990s. Software went from a hidden expense created internally to a fixed functional specification. Companies were looking to buy as much software as they could. Because companies were (and still are) writing software, packaged solutions became an expensive adjunct to standard operating procedures. This was big business that *everyone* wanted to get in on.

OTHER SPENDING ACCELERATORS

Just when it appeared the software business would slow, Y2K became another corporate initiative that accelerated spending. Conditioned by Gartner's widely quoted, back-of-the-envelope estimates of a $300-billion-plus cost worldwide to fix this problem, information technologists accelerated their ERP system deployments. Hoards of programmers and consultants were hired to audit, track down, and repair potential system problems. IT budgets expanded, and spending continued to accelerate.

After Y2K, another phenomenon took hold: the Internet. An entirely new set of infrastructure, applications, and tools was thrown to buyers with the expectation that companies would eat it up. For a while, they did. *Clicks & Bricks, the New Economy, Internet time*, and other slogans became the watchwords for companies. Web-based applications and web sites consumed time and money. All of the "old" technology architectures that were just beginning to function properly were "bad," and anything that was on the Web was "good." Any corporation without a plan for the Web was criticized by analysts and Wall Street. Corporations were forced to crank out more capital and increase budgets for IT.

By 2001, corporations had had enough. The economy slowed, and so did IT spending. Corporations began examining their assets—what they were using and what they weren't.

Gartner and Y2K

The research organization of Gartner that serves buyers of technology has historically relied on a qualitative rather than a quantitative style of research and analysis. This characteristic was all too evident in its initial estimates for the costs to remedy the "Year 2000 Problem," better known as Y2K. The problem was simple: Because many computer systems were not designed to accommodate four-digit years, there was the possibility of computer-system malfunctions, some of which could have had serious economic and social consequences. Gartner analyst Kevin Schick derived a financial estimate of the problem through general knowledge of how many lines of software (in particular, COBOL) existed in the world, the percentage of those lines that were date dependent, and the cost per line to repair the damage. The estimate was accurate within an order of magnitude. It is still open to interpretation whether the ensuing hype had similar accuracy.

THE SOFTWARE DECADE

The 1990s should be called the software decade. During this time, software went from being an equal component to one that dominated IT spending.[10] From 1990 to 2000, the allocation of capital to software increased from 28 to 45 percent. Every other category (even communications) decreased, as you can see in the next figure.

Before 1990, most software was built by users or bundled with hardware. The largest independent software companies (including MSA, Dun & Bradstreet, and Computer Associates) had revenues below $500 million. Only Microsoft ($1.2 billion) and IBM ($10 billion estimated in software) had software revenues in excess of $1 billion.[11] At the time, Microsoft was not considered a key supplier to corporations, and much of IBM's software was bundled into its proprietary hardware. Users had few other choices.

Most software investments were for customized, homegrown applications built by internal staff and consultants. In 1990, only 26 percent of all software solutions were purchased.[12] But this changed dramatically over the next 11 years. By 2002, some 35 percent of all corporate software was purchased. The remaining 65 percent was split evenly between custom software built by third parties and software solutions built with in-house resources.

This complexity created the need for software that would integrate custom and packaged solutions, manage performance, and manage networks on which the applications would run. With every software package and market came functional and technological shortcomings that precipitated new software packages. This fueled sales growth and the salaries of programmers who could install and modify these packages.

Software programmers and specialists in applications, such as SAP, PeopleSoft, and Oracle, as well as in generic technology, including C++ and Visual Basic, were able to command high wages by the mid- to late 1990s. Contract programmers via large consulting companies were costing corporations over $1,000 a day. Freelance programmers could make $200,000 to $300,000 per year, and a kid out of college with hot skills could quickly reach a six-figure salary with a major corporation.

The combination of ERP, enterprise software, Y2K, and the Internet caused the stoking of salaries and shortages of good

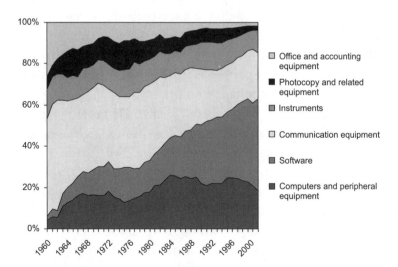

Corporate IT spending breakout by type. Over the past 40 years, spending has shift-ed dramatically between different investment areas of IT. Software has gone from being the smallest sector to being the largest, followed by communications and computer/peripheral equipment. *Source: BEA.*

software talent, adding to overall costs in the 1990s. While buyers would not readily admit it, they started to become concerned over escalating costs. In particular, they grew tired of the big-bang software projects, too many of which led to huge financial consequences rather than an increase in productivity. Although many companies suffered, a few buyers came out on top—and they have much in common.

Spending behaviors

Companies can be grouped according to spending behaviors. Victor, the pharmaceutical client mentioned at the beginning of this chapter, had a history of buying technology without seeking a strong correlation to business benefits. He focused on getting a budget for new technological endeavors. Other clients followed alternative paths.

Ernesto was a different type of client. In late 2002, he had just finished installing a new web procurement package. He took my advice, waited six months to buy the software, and was able to get it at a 90 percent discount. Ernesto's company, in the consumer packaged goods industry, needed to make significant changes to the product and ended up with a fairly customized package. (While it was likely that the company he purchased his software from would be going out of business, it didn't matter because he was able to obtain the product's source code and change it at will.) Ernesto supported the package with a new development group in India—an approach that should save him over $1 million a year in IT costs and cut company procurement costs even more.

Ernesto is one of my favorite types of clients. He never jumps on the latest technology bandwagon, and he waits for the right moment to invest. He didn't make big investments in ERP in the 1990s, though he did get a pretty good ERP system from QAD, an ERP software company based in California. QAD's package is simple to install and doesn't cost much to maintain. Ernesto patched his other systems in a minimal way to get through Y2K and didn't do much on the Internet until the smoke cleared and all the fashionably gullible had burnt through a lot of money. He gets a lot from his technology with minimal spending.

And then there is William.

William is a client who doesn't want to spend any money on technology. He runs a small chemical plant and spends less than 0.5 percent of his revenues on IT. When I last spoke with him, he still had an old BPCS system from SSA running on AS/400s. He changed some dates in date-sensitive systems to become Y2K compliant and set up a rudimentary presence on the Web while his competitors did much more. According to recent financial reports, William's conservative attitude hasn't helped his business, but it hasn't hurt it either.

William sees IT as an operating expense that should be minimized. He views technology as something he consumes, like oil or electricity, and he manages it accordingly. William has never done anything remarkable with technology; his company has experienced unremarkable financial performance.

These three clients represent different parts of the IT spending triangle, illustrated in the figure below. Ernesto is very careful in his IT spending, while William is more reluctant. Victor, the biggest client of the three, was not interested in my advice because it didn't support

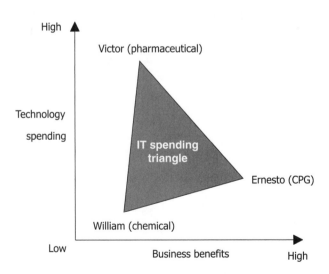

The IT spending triangle. The clients represent several buyer behaviors. Victor has followed popular technology trends and installed a large number of systems at high costs. William spends the least and gets the least from technology. Ernesto has taken a slower approach than Victor in his adoption of technology but gets more bang for his buck. All technology buyers fall somewhere in the IT spending triangle defined by these three clients.

his decision. These three clients define the technology spending extremes of the past few decades. Unfortunately, most companies in the 1990s acted more like Victor than Ernesto or William.

THE RESULT

The IT buying extravagances of the 1990s were the inevitable result of an unflagging faith in technology—a faith that has been a strength and chronic weakness of the United States. That faith is about to be tested.

During the ups and downs of the late 20th century, IT became the assumed driver to corporate profitability and prosperity. Spending increased dramatically. Adding technology system after technology system had the effect of reconfiguring corporate behavior and spending patterns. Spending on technology was supposed to facilitate change, and it did—but at a great price. That price was an increased reliance on software that varied greatly in cost and effectiveness.

Corporations found themselves on shifting ground. Software paced the growth of the last decade, and software and its associated and unpredictable costs have made many companies wake up and reexamine how they might deploy technology in the future. That future is already here.

CHAPTER THREE

L E S S   B A N G
F O R   T H E   I T   B U C K

Hershey Foods Corp., citing problems in the rollout of technol-
ogy, said it expects to lose up to $150 million in sales this year
[1999] and miss Wall Street's earnings estimates by as much as
10 percent.

—Wall Street Journal[1]

E XUBERANCE FOR THE NEW has always been a linchpin of Western civilization. This love, like tragedy in a Greek play, has at times been taken to fatal excess. The last decade of software spending served up some key signs of this.

The 1990s was the decade for big software projects. Corporations shifted their buying focus from hardware to software and from building to buying software applications. This shift came close to breaking the backs of clients and the relationships they had with consultants like myself.

"I need you to write a letter to our board of directors," said Frank, CIO of a large Midwest services company. "We did the math, and the only way we can justify the system is to write it off over 13 years. I need you to confirm this in writing."

This was not something I was prepared to do or even *could* do. I was concerned about the path Frank had chosen for this ERP project—a fast, "big-bang" implementation that would consume lots of money before we even knew if it was the right path. It was a risky endeavor with few rewards. For such a large system, a depreciation of seven or eight years was the only limit that could be prudently considered. Still, Frank wanted that letter.

"Look. There is no way I can get this funded unless you do this for me," Frank said. "I've already spent $12 million on the software. I need a lot more to get it installed. You can't leave me hanging like this!"

He was growing more agitated. He saw that a letter from an "expert" to make his budget-busting implementation fit corporate rules and guidelines would not be coming, at least not from me. He told me that if I wouldn't sign a letter, he would find someone who would, and that this wasn't the type of service he expected as a client.

I told him that I couldn't in good conscience write that letter. It was against corporate policy. He hung up. I never heard back from Frank.

Frank, and many others, never fully considered the details of installing and managing large technology implementations before jumping into the buying pool.

SOFTWARE BUYING PATTERNS

These discussions were all too common in the 1990s. Another such discussion revolved around whether a client in the financial industry would select PeopleSoft or SAP for its worldwide back-office system. A meeting was set up: SAP would present in the morning and PeopleSoft in the afternoon. Both were given business processes to emulate. Performance at the meeting would determine which vendor the company selected.

SAP's team came in and went through their standard live demonstration using their confusing and timeworn user interface. Little focus or attention was given to what the client initially asked for, but with a little prodding, it was easy to see that SAP had the functionality required to meet the needs of the client. The SAP sales-people were far from personable. They were arrogant and believed they had the business.

The PeopleSoft team cruised in after lunch and started handing out gifts: coffee mugs, bags, hats, and T-shirts. They had an upbeat, modern-looking graphical presentation that focused exactly on what the client needed. Everyone loved what PeopleSoft did and how the team communicated its message. Overall, the client was enamored with PeopleSoft and its software. But I spotted some-thing worth mentioning.

"Did anyone notice the logo on the software demonstrated?" I asked. "It was Excel." No one responded. Perhaps others had noticed it but did not want to speak up. PeopleSoft had created a demonstration system in Microsoft Excel that used data extracted from its software package. It had written some simple software mac-ros in Excel to illustrate the client's business process. Everything the client liked about PeopleSoft was more of an extension of Excel than of PeopleSoft.

There were also two significant functional gaps in the PeopleSoft application that would force a change in the client's rollout sched-ule. SAP, on the other hand, had all the necessary functionality with its "what you see is what you get" presentation. If the client picked PeopleSoft, the initial specification and delivery schedule would have to be changed. The client thanked me for my observations and chose PeopleSoft.

This was what it was like to buy software in the 1990s. Many companies ignored the difficult details of what it would take to ulti-mately get systems working. Such approaches proved inherently risky. If implementations went wrong, they could "go dead" instead of "going live." Or they could be well over budget. Or both. And more times than people care to remember, they did. The buying patterns of the 1990s laid the foundation for today's slowdown and reevaluation of buying patterns.

Still growing

Software is the only investment sector of IT that has continued to grow from 2000 to 2002. As discussed in chapter 2, the succession of ERP, Y2K, and Internet initiatives fueled the extreme software market growth of the last decade. This led to large shifts in how IT dollars were spent. Much more was being spent on third-party services and software providers than in the past. Software became not only the driver but the leader of technology spending growth.

As the figure below shows, prepackaged software applications made up the fastest-growing area of spending over the last 30 years. This growth fueled the amount of money companies spent internally and externally to customize packages to better fit business needs. Even though companies were buying more software packages, they still spent more money on the customized labor required to make them work. In many ways, packaged software accelerated rather than slowed IT spending.

These factors have helped to fuel the staggering growth of the software market. This growth is even more remarkable when this same data is plotted using a logarithmic scale, as in the figure on the next page. Logarithmic scales illustrate growth as a function of

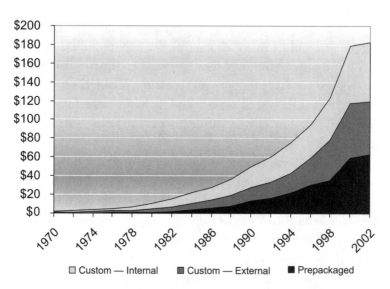

□ Custom — Internal   ■ Custom — External   ■ Prepackaged

U.S. business investment in software between 1970 and 2002 ($ billions, actual).[2] This figure represents what U.S. companies capitalized on new software each year. Business investment in software consists of three components: prepackaged, custom-external, and custom-internal. Prepackaged software can be installed on computers and run with little change or modification. Custom-external represents the monies spent on contractors and nonemployees to build new software or modify prepackaged software. Custom-internal represents the cost of employees used to build new software or modify prepackaged software. *Source: BEA.*

magnitude, which has held surprisingly constant for software. Using a log scale, software spending has consistently increased in any given 14- to 16-year period until 2000.

Obviously, this growth trend cannot continue using any economic measure. Consider the following:

- If IT spending were to grow at the same aggressive rate of the 1990s (1992 to 2000), then it would represent slightly more than 70 percent of total U.S. capital spending by 2010.

- If software spending growth were to continue at the same growth rate of the last 30 years, then U.S. companies would invest more than $1 trillion in software by 2010.

Clearly, neither of these scenarios is possible. Even as business units are adding to IT expenditures through purchases that are expensed instead of capitalized, the money that has fueled software growth cannot flow as it has in the past. The natural laws of economics dictate that such investments must decelerate. Beyond natural laws, another factor has emerged to temper spending enthusiasm.

Disturbing stories

As IT spending continued to climb during the late 1990s, disturbing stories began to emerge. The potential benefits of technology were overshadowed by the inability of sellers to quantify those benefits.

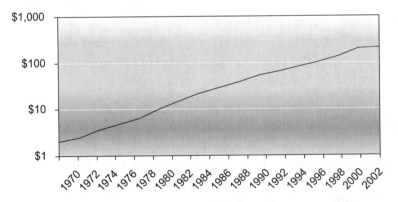

Private business investment in software (in $ billions, actual). Capitalized software spending plotted on a logarithmic scale shows steady growth over the last 30 years. Unfortunately for the software vendors selling to corporations, this growth is not sustainable. *Source: BEA.*

Show me the references

One of the biggest problems that buyers of technology continue to have, even with established vendors, involves reference accounts. Most software vendors are often unable (or unwilling) to supply a customer account (or an analyst firm) with a well-prepared list of references that would illustrate how well (or how badly) their software functioned for a certain type of business process. During the 1990s, even the most rudimentary of references were rarely given to buyers looking for technological proof points. References are important to companies purchasing software for two important reasons: They give an indication of whether the software in question can accommodate the automation of the business process desired and whether the software can process all needed transactions and data in a reasonable timeframe.

And the dark side of large enterprise software purchasing reared its ugly head when budget overruns and poor IT implementations started to crop up in the press.

This bad press accelerated in the late 1990s when the Internet craze took hold. Consider these sample headlines:

- **Consultant, ERP Firm Faces Lawsuit over HR Application** (*InfoWorld*, October 29, 1999): W. L. Gore file[d] a lawsuit against Deloitte & Touche and PeopleSoft over an implementation of PeopleSoft's human resources package.

- **P&G System Is Causing Flawed Data** (*Wall Street Journal*, November 20, 1999): An internally built information repository named SourceOne was reported to deliver faulty cost-allocation data.

- **Home Depot Cuts Off Orders for Whirlpool** (*Wall Street Journal*, January 24, 2000): Whirlpool's launch of SAP caused the loss of orders and mistaken shipments. Home Depot stopped ordering appliances from Whirlpool and sought replacements from other appliance makers.

- Online Order System Snafus Blamed for 50% Drop in 1999 Net Income (*ComputerWorld*, February 15, 2000): For Thomas & Betts, an electronics manufacturer, more than $60 million of business was affected due to a faulty customized order-management system launch.

- Lower Profit at Nike Blamed on i2 Software (*Information Week*, February 28, 2001): During an analyst's call, Nike CEO Philip Knight cited deployment problems of a $400 million supply-chain and demand-chain project, using i2 as a cornerstone for a loss of $80 million to $100 million in sales and a loss in profits of 1 cent per share.

- Top 10 Corporate Information Technology Failures (*ComputerWorld*, October 30, 2000): This list from *ComputerWorld* includes companies such as AMR Corp., FoxMeyer Corp., W. W. Grainger Inc., Greyhound Lines Inc., Hershey Foods Corp., Norfolk Southern Corp., Oxford Health Plans Inc., Snap-On Inc., Tri-Valley Growers, Universal Oil Products LLC, and others. The failures all shared a common theme: They negatively impacted the involved companies, causing massive losses/write-offs because of bungled technology implementations. Some were particularly embarrassing.

ERP HORROR STORIES

On the front page of the *Wall Street Journal* two days before Halloween 1999 was this headline: "Hershey's Biggest Dud Has Turned Out to Be Its New Technology. At the Worse Possible Time, It Can't Fill Its Orders Even as Inventory Grows." Hershey had decided to replace its old order-management and inventory system in 1996 with one designed by SAP. But after spending $112 million on the project, Hershey found that things were going terribly wrong and that distributors were not getting the candy they ordered.

These problems continued into the Christmas season. Hershey missed financial targets for a number of quarters. The company has since been able to repair the problems, and today SAP's software is accurately managing order flow and inventory. Hershey had to pull itself out of a deep hole.

Another company experienced an even worse problem.

In 1994, FoxMeyer Corp. decided to swap out a mainframe-based solution for SAP's R/3 ERP package running on client-server technology. This was a large gamble for a complex project with short implementation times and anticipated fast paybacks. After attempting to go live in 1996, the company was unable to fulfill orders. Later in the year, the once $5 billion company filed for bankruptcy and was eventually sold for $80 million to McKesson Corp., its largest competitor. Management put a large percentage of the blame on the failed IT implementation.[3]

A similar list of snafus could be taken from the dot.com era, though not nearly as much money was wasted by buyers via poor technology implementations. The real losses were in venture and public market investments, where billions of dollars were collectively squandered by such companies as Webvan (home delivery of groceries), Boo.com (high-fashion e-tailer), and Pets.com (animal trinkets and food on the Web), as well as countless software companies that are barely surviving today.

Some companies—Lands' End, Harrah's, and Dell Computers—were able to take advantage of the Internet by moving slowly and investing carefully.

A wakeup call

All of these examples brought the attention of top management to the rarified world of IT. Without any standard metrics for quality or quantification, finger-pointing set in. Rather than rhapsodize over one technology or another, IT managers were forced to start paying closer attention to the business and cost of technology.

"We never got anything from the hundreds of millions we spent on [software] technology in the 1990s," said one CFO of a Fortune 100 company. "IT drove everything, and the business people had little input. But I think we have learned our lesson. Money will never be that loose again."

In one sense, people may have been overreacting. IT failures will always occur. However, they were indicative of a concentrated and widespread set of problems (though more extreme) that all clients had with installing complex technologies in the 1990s. Delays, missing functionality, performance issues, missed going-live dates, and other problems were daily gripes from clients. There were no easy solutions to the problems they faced.

Today, corporate focus is more about responsibility and results than about new technology. This change is being picked up and promulgated by a majority of management magazines, which went from a mindless approval of new technology in the 1990s, to a cautious pragmatism in the late 2000–01, to outright hostility in 2002–03. These fluctuations may be a foreshadowing of things to come.

CORPORATE HABITS ARE HARD TO BREAK

Balancing the cost of changing people's behaviors against the cost of changing software to address business needs became (and still is) a major issue within most corporations. It is easier to change software to accommodate business processes than it is to change corporate behavior to accommodate software. A group of corporate controllers brought this point home to me during a visit to their facility.

I was brought into the corporate headquarters of a major beverage company to moderate a meeting between the financial chiefs of the different divisions. The purpose of the meeting was to agree on certain processes and business structures that could be standardized across the corporation worldwide. Within the first 30 minutes of the meeting, an intellectual fight broke out concerning the concept of a standard chart of accounts.[4]

The controllers insisted passionately that their view of the company should be adopted by all. After they spent the first 90 minutes getting everything off their minds, they attempted to create impractical structures that could accommodate everything. I was worried that the meeting would bog down and become a waste of time. It was time for a process check.

We went around the table and asked each person the most important thing that the company could focus on. The group agreed that customers were the most important. I then asked about the simplest way we could deliver a chart of accounts to help the customers with the software they had selected. Ten minutes later we were on to the next item.

There were a thousand meetings like this where companies made decisions to come up with highly customized business processes rather than first consider those provided by software vendors. The result was to take standard software and customize it to such a degree that little remained of the standardized package. In a sense, application software packages became ungainly toolkits with high customization costs and high risks for failures. This variation led to massive swings in consulting costs, and budget estimates that were much too low. The chart on this page shows the results of a Gartner report that examined cost overruns for typical customers.

As the chart illustrates, buying and implementing enterprise software was only the beginning of cost overruns. It is no accident that many software vendors today are trying to make their software easier to install and maintain long term; they are also looking to capture

	Hardware	Systems Software	Application Software	External Services	Internal Staff	Overhead Allocation
Plan	N/A	N/A	N/A	Well-planned	Well-planned	Underbudgeted 40–75%
Acquire	Underbudgeted 10–30%	Underbudgeted 10–30%	Well-planned	Well-planned	Underbudgeted 10–30%	Underbudgeted 40–75%
Implement - Pilot - Rollout	Underbudgeted 10–30%	Underbudgeted 10–30%	Well-planned	Underbudgeted 10–30%	Underbudgeted 40–75%	Underbudgeted 40–75%
Maintain - Year 1 - Year 2 - Year n	Underbudgeted 10–30%	Underbudgeted 40–75%	Well-planned	Underbudgeted 40–75%	Underbudgeted 10–30%	Underbudgeted 40–75%
Major upgrade - Rel 1 - Rel n	Underbudgeted 40–75%	Underbudgeted 40–75%	Underbudgeted 10–30%	Underbudgeted 40–75%	Underbudgeted 40–75%	Underbudgeted 40–75%

Legend:
- Well-planned by most users
- Costs underbudgeted by 10% to 30%
- Costs underbudgeted by 40% to 75%

Gartner Inc. examined various aspects of the total cost of ownership (TCO) for enterprise packages in the late 1990s.[5] Based on conversations with clients, systems integrators, and software vendors, it devised this chart tracking cost overruns for typical customers. Needless to say, the average customer was way over budget for enterprise software in the 1990s. *Source: Gartner Inc.*

additional services revenue. Users found that an expensive-to-install system was equally expensive to maintain. Companies are better at estimating and managing these costs today. As you'll see in chapter 5, buyers came to recognize that the advantages software gives customers were being outweighed by the cost of maintaining it.

Customization is a long tradition in IT shops. While many people believe that few companies write their own software anymore, customization continues to represent the major share of business investment for software, as the figure below shows. In 1970, there was not much of a prepackaged software industry. In 1980, prepackaged software represented only 10 percent of all expenditures. By 1990, that number reached nearly 20 percent.

The packaged software industry took off in the early 1990s. So did the number of publicly named failures. This does not imply that implementing a homegrown package is less risky than implementing a prepackaged one. In the late 1980s, one of my clients in the automotive industry spent more than $150 million on an aborted launch of a software package that was supposed to automate all the operations of its worldwide manufacturing plants. During the early 1990s, another client in the food industry attempted to launch a similar program to the tune of $50 million. Such mammoth failures were not unknown in the IT world. (Problems with internal software development projects have been well documented in such books as *The Mythical Man-Month: Essays on Software Engineering*, by Frederick P. Brooks, first published in 1975.)

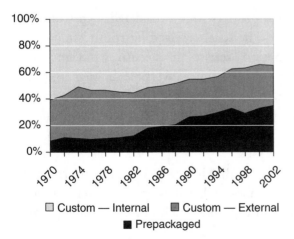

Business investment of software by type between 1970 and 2002. Over the last 30 years, companies have shifted a significant portion of internal-development efforts toward buying software. Little has changed in spending for external services as a percentage of the total.[6] *Source: BEA.*

A custom software solution is built exactly to the specification of the customer. A prepackaged solution must either be used as-is out of the box or customized to meet the needs of the customer. There has been a constant battle between a company's need to implement its own customized business processes and its need to find ones that are standardized and prepackaged within a software application.

Customization vs. standardization

The battle between customization and standardization added to cost overruns. In the beginning, most IT managers and CIOs shrugged off the conflicts and cost overruns as part of the learning process. A $35 million project that came in at $70 million was a "success" as long as the system eventually worked.

These large cost overruns fostered a fundamental lack of trust between technology vendors, technologists, and the executives who were paying the bills. Many technology vendors operated under the view that it was easier to ask for forgiveness than to receive permission, users overlooked key details that were essential to the success of projects, and consultants and systems integrators pushed large projects regardless of the bills and usefulness to the client.

When companies bought software based on emotion or tradition rather than fact, they usually found themselves scrambling at the eleventh hour; core pieces of functionality wound up missing, thus requiring customized and expensive links to existing systems. Because these existing systems were not decommissioned, costs and complexity soared.

Believe it or not, such projects were considered successful—and in many ways they were. The seller received fat commission checks for salespeople and fat option exercises for executives and employees. The consultants succeeded with huge overtime billings and large bonuses for partners managing a practice. The direct buyers won because they were able to build a large staff, have clout within their companies, and use the project experience as a launching pad for higher salaries and better jobs.

The losers were companies that had to pay for cost overruns and live with disappointments about what these projects were supposed to do for their bottom and top lines. Such problems came home to roost as companies increased their spending on IT as well as their dependence and financial exposure to failure.

As IT consumed more of the budget, it created more risks. The desire to move to prepackaged software was driven by the belief that buying software was less risky than building it.

BIG BILLS, BIG SPILLS

The 1990s were unique because so many companies attempted so many large IT projects in a short time. This resulted in an unprecedented number of IT project failures that were publicized—and an even larger number of private ones. Companies are still recovering from this fallout. It has affected corporate buying behavior, changed the IT evaluation process, and created a high degree of cynicism about IT within corporations.

The view of technology illustrated in the figure below does not include the *benefits* of the 1990s, such as increased automation of key processes to cut costs or the ability to better target customers, but rather encompasses the expensive, painful, and sometimes fruitless pursuit of those benefits. A $30 million cost overrun overshadowed a $50 million benefit down the line because the return on investment was too long in coming. Many of the large IT projects implemented in the 1990s were essential to keep businesses functioning and serving their clients.

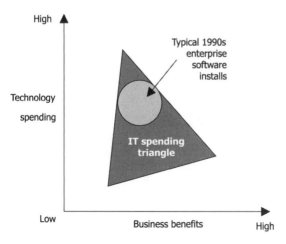

IT buyer behavior. Many implementations of large enterprise systems during the 1990s fell into the upper reaches of the IT spending triangle. Companies do not want to repeat the mistakes they made in the 1990s and are avoiding large and risky IT expenditures.

Managers who spearheaded IT projects during the 1990s stopped companies from malfunctioning because of Y2K issues, helped companies better manage their inventory and customers, and improved the efficiency of complex supply chains because of better scheduling and planning. Through the development of web-based applications, they slashed the cost of taking an order via self-service, lowered their cost of deploying applications, and gave customers and suppliers unthinkable visibility and access to information that would help them greatly.

However, because of the large amount of money companies are spending on IT, the fundamental issue for many is shifting from the benefits derived from technology to the ultimate cost of technology. For example, the META Group, an IT research organization based in Stamford, CT, released a report in 2003 titled "Deriving Value from 21st Century ERP Applications" 13 years after the concept was created. Quantitative answers and value are hard to find.

SURVIVAL GUIDE
FOR BUYERS

PURCHASING IT

Before attempting to implement large, complex projects, buyers should first consider the following:

- **Big projects have big risks.** Failure is easy; success is hard—especially for large, complex IT projects. To be successful, companies must enter into a big project with realistic expectations, a business rationale for the project, a technological advisor to ensure that the project can be executed, and strong diligence. Today, companies implement large projects on a step-like basis to minimize risk and maximize success.

- **Project management, project management, project management.** The success or failure of any large technology installation is project management. Technology knowledge is not as important as operational capabilities. Before throwing money and resources at a large project, project leaders should first analyze the reasons for the problems and best determine how they should be resolved. Sometimes the best measures are to halt the project, regroup, and start anew.

- **References, references, references.** References are as important as project management. Companies need to get the seller to share references from other customers. References from different categories (such as functionality, technical performance, and stability) as well as industry fit should be examined. Any company that cannot offer references should be considered a risky prospect.

- **Sellers may not have your best interest in mind.** There are still many Three-Card Monte schemes being played by sellers who look to grab the money and run. Most sales forces are compensated to deliver large, up-front license fees and will look to sign contracts that lock you into a payment schedule that cannot be changed. For large

SURVIVAL GUIDE
FOR BUYERS

projects, hold back funds and release monies based on the successful completion of milestones.

- **Large projects are not a sprint for IT, but a marathon of upkeep and expense.** Big projects have big bills down the line. These costs include the addition of extra licenses as the business grows, technology and functional upgrades, the cost of integration, user training, and other expenses. If you can't afford the initial price tag, then you probably can't afford the long-term upkeep of the project. Ensure that the benefits will be long term and in sync with business plans and directions.

- **Get experience, buy experience.** Large projects are like the big leagues: You need the very best players (who come at a price) to win. Hire key players who have successfully implemented these types of projects. In the 1990s, management information systems (MIS) folks were being asked to manage budgets and projects that were more complex than anything they had done in the past. This caused problems. Be realistic about the people chosen to manage large enterprise software projects.

SURVIVAL GUIDE
FOR SELLERS

SELLING IT

If sellers want their customers to be successful at the lowest possible cost, they should consider the previous points as well as the following:

- **Don't overpromise.** One of the biggest challenges for sellers of technology is not to exaggerate the benefits and capabilities of their products. Asking for forgiveness rather than getting permission (or fully disclosing) will get you in trouble in the new IT buying environment. New buyers will not tolerate fundamental misrepresentation of product capabilities. Reorient and train your sales force to aggressively, but accurately, sell the real value of your solution. If the products are not ready for general release, look for early customers that will act as your beta sites and inform them as such.

- **Pick your customers carefully.** The best customer is not necessarily the one that will give you a check for your product. A good customer has a fundamental business problem that will be addressed by your technology. Don't let customers drag you down a path that is away from the fundamental focus of your company because they have cash on hand. Consider how well suited the customer's organization is to your particular solution. If a big business process change is required for effective use of your technology, proceed with caution and only if upper management is committed to making such changes occur.

- **Focus on client success.** This may sound obvious, but there are few incentives that can be used to ensure that a customer successfully uses a given product well. Too much "drive-buy selling" looking for quick revenue creates an environment that looks only at the short term. Unless sellers change compensation and reward metrics for corporate officers and other customer-facing

SURVIVAL GUIDE
FOR SELLERS

employees, client success stories will be haphazard rather than commonplace.

- **Simplify complexity.** The more complexity within a project, the greater likelihood for problems and possible failure. Sellers should minimize rather than maximize the complexity of how their solutions fit into the IT portfolio of buyers. Chapters 6 and 11 will discuss how sellers can reduce complexity to improve their chances of success in the market.

CHAPTER FOUR

SHOW ME THE PRODUCTIVITY

...information technologies have begun to alter the manner in which we do business and create value, often in ways not readily foreseeable even five years ago...and, as a consequence, [have] apparently added to growth of multifactor productivity, and thus to labor productivity acceleration.

—Alan Greenspan, Chairman,
Federal Reserve Board[1]

I calculated that the total amount of time that humans have waited for web pages to load cancels out all of the productivity gains of the information age.

—Dilbert, IT worker cartoon character[2]

W HEN IT COMES TO IT, getting experts to agree on the meaning of productivity or return is far from easy. But given the amount of IT spending that occurs, coming to an agreement on these definitions is important to the future of IT. Like all large corporate investments, IT projects must deliver some type of return. Calculating this return is not always easy. In the mid-1990s, one client, Mary, asked what she could expect as a return on investment (ROI) from replacing her base financial and order-management software. The answer was not simple.

The solution she was looking to replace was over 10 years old, and the vendor that had sold it to her company was ceasing support. This meant that it would become increasingly expensive to maintain and run the system if any changes, either technological or functional, were needed. She was also beginning to consider the effect of Y2K on her company. In addition, because her company was beginning to expand, the older systems were increasingly unable to handle the increased volume of business. Mary didn't want to run the risk of an unsupported and inflexible piece of software and decided it was time for a change.

For Mary, the ROI or productivity gains from the new software were not clear. What *was* clear, however, was the future risk of failure and the potential of not being able to take an order or close the financial books of the corporation. If the older system could continue to serve the needs of the business, then there would be no need to change systems.

Mary's choice came down to managing risk, but she was told by management that the justification of the systems needed to have a classic ROI component. A long conversation finally came to a head.

"So when all is said and done, your new system will allow you to continue to do what you have been doing when you first implement it. After you figure out some of the bells and whistles, you may get some additional benefits from it," I said. "Using a classic definition of ROI, you initially get nothing. Your return is negative. But better use in the future may get you into positive territory."

"Hmmm. So what you are saying is that there would be no ROI for three to five years, right?" she replied.

WHY INVEST IN IT?

Information technology has huge *potential*. It can help a company increase revenues and overall productivity. But as I pointed out in chapter 3, there is a great divide between the actual returns on a technology investment and the potential returns. Companies have built strategies where IT is a cornerstone. Others save millions of dollars in inventory and labor while spending a fraction of that. Still others have unwittingly accomplished the opposite and made decisions that have squandered millions of dollars. Results depend on the approach chosen and who is using the tool of IT.

Most companies spend money on technology to enhance their overall competitive position and productivity. But many IT investments do not fall into this category.

Mary, for example, had little choice. She had to either buy a new system or put her company on the brink of not being able to take an order. Although she couldn't get a good ROI or productivity metric to show her boss, she made a good decision to minimize risk for the company. Many technologies are purchased with these factors in mind. Companies invest heavily in different types of IT "plumbing" (e.g., network management, storage management, security, recovery and backup systems) to keep IT systems afloat. Without such systems, businesses could grind to a halt.

And then there are the purchases that are made because of competitive pressures. As IT has matured and expanded, there are many pressures to maintain technological parity with your competition. If your competitor is offering online order tracking and you cannot, you may lose business. So what do you do? You spend $250,000 to meet the competitive pressure and install online tracking.

Companies buy technology for a number of good reasons, some of which have nothing to do with a business or productivity gain but everything to do with minimizing business or technological risks. Companies should have an easily quantifiable measure that their investments are providing a corporate benefit, when you consider that nearly 50 percent of all capital goods spending is on IT. The big one that economists, stock pickers, and corporate executives use is productivity.

Finding a relationship between productivity and IT spending should not be difficult. Both common and professional opinion states that IT investments are key to productivity growth in the United States. Some simple examples show us the reasons for this view. Taking an order over the Web can cost a company between 30 cents and $1.00, while a person taking the same order over the phone can cost as much as $35. The use of technology and its associated advantages in this case is an example of a well-defined, bounded project with a clear productivity benefit: reduction of labor cost. Many other examples exist where technology shows a positive productivity benefit for companies. Given the importance of technology and the large amount of corporate investment made in technology, it should be simple to determine its total impact on productivity. Wrong again. Consider the following:

- Most economic studies examining the area of IT-related productivity are inconclusive at best.

- Independent market reviews of key products or vendors related to corporate initiatives, including CRM and SCM, state that a minority of buyers realize benefits from technology.[3]

- Few sellers of technology have ROI or productivity metrics that are convincing.

These issues will continue to slow technology spending. Buyers have begun to understand that the larger consideration for technology purchases is not *if* IT assists productivity, but rather *when* IT delivers benefits.

The productivity paradox

The impact of IT on productivity is unclear. This "productivity paradox" was triggered by a quip made in a *New York Review of Books* article in 1987 when Nobel-prize winning economist Robert Solow wrote, "You can see the computer age everywhere except in the productivity statistics."[4]

While productivity sounds like an arcane concept (and is often approached as such by economists and research houses), it is actually simple. It is all about getting more for less. If you pay a worker $10 per hour and he produces 5 percent more widgets this year than last, then labor productivity has increased by 5 percent. The use of technology can be a factor in this increase—or not. It all depends.

A more complex view—and one that some (such as Alan Greenspan) believe to be more accurate—is multifactor productivity.

Multifactor productivity not only considers the labor cost of $10 per hour and the 5 percent increase in output, but also any capital expenditures (of which IT is a substantial portion). So multifactor productivity represents the difference between the change in company outputs (what is sold) and the change in company inputs (what is spent). Standard productivity measurements only look at the labor (as the input) against all outputs. It is a less complex view than multifactor productivity and the one used and considered by financial markets.

Points and counterpoints

These productivity measurements and their interpretation set the stage for point and counterpoint arguments that continue to this day. Research concerning IT and its impact on productivity includes the following:

- Nicholas Carr, "IT Doesn't Matter," *Harvard Business Review.* May 2003. This report created a stream of controversy when released because it asserts that IT is not strategically important to companies in the future and must be managed like any commodity, such as power or telephone service. Carr asserts that IT budgets should be slashed to pursue only projects that promote simple blocking and tackling of business problems.

- McKinsey & Co., "Understanding the Contribution of IT Relative to Other Factors," October 2001.[5] This report looks at 59 sectors in the industry and comes to the conclusion that most of the IT-driven productivity gains between 1995 and 2000 were concentrated in six sectors: computer assembly, retail, securities (financial), semiconductor manufacturing, telecommunications, and wholesale. These groups represented 30 percent of the total private sector.

- Federal Reserve Board, *Information Technology and Productivity: Where Are We Now and Where Are We Going?* May 10, 2002.[6] This report updates one published in 2000 and looks at productivity gains between 1995 and 2001. It concludes that a high percentage of productivity gains can be attributed to the production of technology (e.g., computers and semiconductors) as well as the use of technology.

- Harvard University and the Federal Reserve Board, *Raising the Speed Limit: U.S. Economic Growth in the Information Age*, May 1, 2000.[7] This study states that the production of IT was a key accelerator of productivity gains in the late 1990s. The study focuses on reasons for and potential continuance of economic growth, not on how well or how badly technology is being used.

- National Bureau of Economic Research. *Does the "New Economy" Measure Up to the Great Inventions of the Past?*, August 2000.[8] This study examines IT in the context of other inventions, such as electricity and the internal combustion engine. It argues that the productivity gains garnered by IT are slight, at best, when compared to these other technological inventions.

- Organisation for Economic Co-operation and Development. *Seizing the Benefits of ICT in a Digital Economy*, 2003.[9] This paper advocates that countries around the world should invest heavily in information and communications technology (ICT) because of the productivity and GDP growth that countries such as the United States have been able to enjoy.

- Strassmann, Inc. Paul Strassmann has been a longtime figure in the economics of IT through his direct involvement in industry

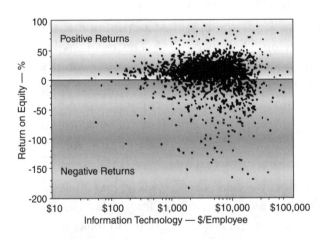

IT and productivity continue to be unrelated. This figure is a plot of 4,000 companies using 2002 financial data; it shows the relationship between return on equity, a commonly used indicator of shareholder return, and technology spending per employee. It illustrates that there is little relationship between IT spending and profitability and productivity. *Source: Strassmann, Inc. 2003.*

and as a senior executive of NASA. His two books, *Information Productivity* (1997) and *The Squandered Computer* (1999), as well as a variety of well-researched studies that can be found on his web site, question any relationship between productivity and IT spending, as shown in the figure on the previous page.[10]

- U.S. Department of Commerce. *Digital Economy 2002*, February 2002.[11] This report states that much of the recent economic progress and growth in the U.S. economy is tightly linked to IT spending and use. One key aspect is the creation of highly paid jobs attached to the servicing and selling of IT.

When all of these studies are compared, a few common themes emerge:

- A high percentage of the overall increase in U.S. productivity is attributed to the growth of the IT industry and price-performance gains of semiconductors, computers, and telecommunications equipment.
- No one can agree on how to measure productivity gains obtained through the use of IT.
- Any productivity gains garnered through the use of technology are highly dependent on how the technology is used.

IT generates its own productivity

A high percentage of the productivity credited to IT can be attributed to its production and sales. Regardless of which productivity metric is examined, the actual production of technology (e.g., making computers, semiconductors, and others) represents around 50 percent of all the productivity claimed by technology. The figure on the next page shows that IT's contribution to productivity wavered under 1 percent for nearly 20 years before exploding in the last 10 years.

According to the Federal Reserve Board, by the mid-1990s more productivity gains were coming from the production than the actual use of IT. This is a relatively recent phenomenon that has slowed along with the IT market. It is an interesting point because the mere existence of technology has a large effect on the government's productivity figures. It is similar to the effect of a black hole on time and space; its presence warps and changes the prior reality. It's not what most people assume "productivity" represents.

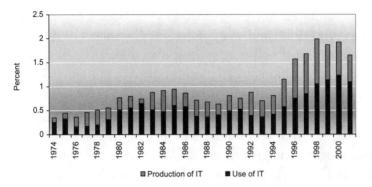

Contributions from the use and production of IT to growth in labor productivity in nonfarm business, 1974–2001. According to statistics from the Federal Reserve Board, IT has had a major impact on the overall productivity of the U.S. economy, sometimes more from its production than its use. *Source: Federal Reserve Board.*

Regardless of which opinion is taken, this figure shows that the U.S. economy and stock prices (all of which are heavily influenced by productivity numbers) are captive to a buying mentality that considers technology an engine of growth. Productivity gains of the future related to the production of technology might be much less if companies start believing that there are better ways to increase their productivity than buying more technology.

MEASURING IT-BASED PRODUCTIVITY

Great disagreement exists over what connotes IT-based productivity or which IT-related metric it is important to measure. As mentioned earlier, the two types of productivity are labor and multifactor. Neither one, however, measures the qualitative benefits of technology. For instance, tracking the delivery status of a book order made over Amazon.com through either the FedEx or United Parcel Service (UPS) web site is not captured as having any productivity value. In fact, just the opposite is true: It represents a consumption of capital without an increase in output, probably even lowering a measurement of productivity. Yet few of us would want to return to a world where we didn't have access via the Web (or other means) to important information and data. In this example, technology betters our lifestyles but does not necessarily help productivity (except for what is represented by the manufacturing of such items). The productivity measurements do not explain when technology is used in an innovative fashion. For example, the web-based auction house eBay has created an entirely new business and many jobs with the technology of the Web.

Technology also includes a convenience factor. We have the perception that it makes our lives better, and we are willing to pay a price for that convenience. But what price are we willing to pay? As Internet-based freebies ranging from music to information to applications are being replaced with for-pay alternatives, people and companies are beginning to quantify the value and worth of technology. Productivity numbers do not capture all the benefits of technology. More of the benefits come from how technology is used.

Company use determines returns

Information technology success or failure is highly attributable to individual company behavior and management. The aforementioned statistics bear out many of the events mentioned in the last chapter as well as my own experiences. In my 25 years in the IT business, I've seen the same clients make the same questionable decisions time and time again. With CIOs swapping chairs biannually, the lack of corporate memory and experience is not surprising. It explains why only a modest number of companies have been able to figure out how to use technology effectively. The computer manufacturing sector is one of high productivity, but effective use of technology differs.

For instance, in 1997, Dell decided to stop its SAP installation against common wisdom. The company saw that the highly integrated approach supported by SAP was counterproductive to its business strategy. This strategy was dependent on selling most of its products over the Web and having highly flexible and configurable business processes. To meet this business need, the company decided to build highly customized systems. In contrast, competitors including Hewlett Packard, IBM, and Sun Microsystems purchased software from SAP and Oracle. Today, Dell is the leading PC manufacturing company in the world and is quickly gaining market share in computer servers.

All of these studies indicate that IT can deliver benefits and value, but not as automatically as technology sellers would like you to believe. No wonder many of the TLA (three-letter acronym) software products coined ERP, CRM, SCM, and so on are being viewed critically by buyers who are much more cautious with new purchases.

Why software won't sell

The malaise in software sales that continued throughout 2003 is due in equal parts to economic problems and failed expectations. As mentioned in chapter 3, in the late 1990s a number of companies were having trouble implementing big software systems. All software vendors became guilty by association when the major ones—SAP, Oracle, PeopleSoft, i2 Technologies, Siebel Systems, and Baan among others—had well-publicized failures. Unfortunately, these stories led to larger sector failures that made questionable the benefits of implementing these technologies.

In 2002, Bryan Stolle, CEO of Agile Software, said, "The thing that kills me is that we actually have references and can prove that our stuff works. But nobody believes us. Must be the company [the software vendors] we keep." Stolle *does* sell software that works. However, it didn't matter in 2002, when few companies could give away software, much less sell it.

Gartner was one of the first market research firms to recognize the failures. In the mid-1990s, it told clients about problems but never publicized the findings beyond its client base. It published a report in December 1996 titled "Why Do More than 50 percent of TES [technology-enabled selling] Projects Fail?" According to the survey, there are three big reasons 55 percent of the Gartner survey base failed to deliver measurable ROI: 1) failure to define metrics; 2) incorrect choice of applications; and 3) failure to involve the customer's sales force in project plans.

These surveys became a way for companies to put their research on the map and remind software vendors that their claims were perhaps stretched. Reports such as these included:

- **CRM failures.** CRM became the dump-on sector for the new millennium. Reports from Gartner, META Group, Butler Group, Datamonitor, and others[12] stated that between 45 and 75 percent of all CRM projects didn't meet initial objectives. Reasons stated in the 1996 Gartner report were commonly used. The lack of good guidelines and standard processes in financial and manufacturing will always make this group of applications hard to implement.

- **ERP failures.** In 2001, Conference Board surveyed 117 companies that had implemented ERP systems. While 82 percent indicated that they were satisfied to some degree, 40 percent of the projects failed to achieve their business case within one year. In 1997, KPMG Canada surveyed a wide range of companies. Of the ones analyzed, 61 percent reported failures in the implementation of ERP systems. Robbins-Gioia surveyed more than 200 companies, and over 50 percent indicated that their ERP implementations were failures.[13]

- **SCM failures.** A Bear, Stearns & Co. survey of more than 100 companies in the third quarter of 2002 revealed that 44 percent had written off any SCM projects within the last 12 months. That figure was up 9 percent from the previous quarter. It's likely this rate will continue to increase because most companies are loath to admit such failures. Typically, they are rationalized and hidden in the budgets and write-downs of other projects. Supply chain vendor i2 Technologies was given particular attention by Nucleus Research, which surveyed 70 i2 Technologies customer references. It was discovered that 55 percent of customers did not believe they had obtained a positive ROI after an average of 2.2 years' use. (Nucleus has published similar damning ROI studies on SAP, Advanced Technology Group [ATG], and other technology vendors.)[14]

- **Overall problems/failures.** One of the primary sources on how IT does not meet its promise is represented by research done by the Standish Group. In 1994, it came out with *The CHAOS Report*,[15] which stated that nearly a third of all IT projects are canceled before completion and that over half of all projects are almost 200 percent over budget. IT implementations have improved in the last decade, with successes doubling to a third of all projects and failures dropping to 15 percent of the total. Cost overruns have also declined significantly.

These reports were a byproduct of the rash of installations during the 1990s, when both buyers and sellers had naive expectations.

This was all part of an environment that focused on success as a function of how *much* companies spent on technology rather than how *wisely* they spent on technology.

IT SPENDING AVERAGES

Most technology research firms release yearly budget surveys of IT indicating how people will spend their money and on what. One of the more insidious parts of this research is average spending on technology by industry. As the figure below shows, different ranges of IT spending exist as a percentage of sales based on type and industry.

The range of IT spending varies from as little as 2 percent of sales for sectors such as retail and wholesale distribution spending to as much as 10 percent for telecommunications services spending. (Ironically, wholesale distribution and retail are two of the six sectors that accounted for most of the productivity gains during the late 1990s, according to the aforementioned McKinsey report.) While

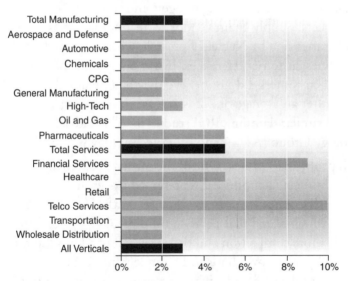

Information technology spending in 2002 by vertical industry. Financial services companies tend to spend the most, whereas certain manufacturing sectors, such as chemicals, tend to spend the least. However, these numbers are meaningless because no correlation exists between how much a company spends and the benefits derived from IT. *Source: AMR Research Inc.*

these surveys were meant to be purely informational, they are also used as benchmarks to rationalize spending levels. For some clients, they become a problem.

"Am I spending enough money here?" asked Charlie, a longtime client in the batch chemical industry. "My CIO says I need to spend a lot more money to modernize my plants, and I think that it is stupid. I'm making money."

Charlie was a smart, pragmatic client with more than 25 years of experience. Whenever I visited his company, I tried to end the day with him so we could go out for a beer and trade war stories. I learned a lot just listening to his often simple and practical way of resolving a problem. He understood his costs and what he got from spending money. He spent less than 0.5 percent of his sales on IT and wanted to keep it that way.

We looked at all the metrics and numbers to help Charlie solve his problem. In the areas of customer satisfaction, inventory turns, quality, and financial returns, Charlie was near the top of his game. There was really nothing that he needed. We kept scratching our heads trying to figure out what Charlie could spend more money on. Nothing was obvious. In frustration, Charlie said, "I bet if this came out of corporate pockets they wouldn't be so fast to spend money." We looked at each other and smiled.

Charlie had unknowingly found the answer. The next day he went back to the CIO and told him that he would be more than happy to upgrade the systems, but corporate had to sign up for all the costs. Corporate would be advanced the saving benefits beyond the current trend line. If the new system were to make operations less efficient, then the difference would be reimbursed to Charlie's facility by corporate.

It worked. Charlie was able to hold spending in line.

Charlie and a few like him are effective users of technology. There is no magic number. They just spend what is required and deploy solutions that help the company generate positive return, through a combination of applying good business sense and technology. This type of attitude is becoming common with CIOs as they are held more accountable for spending and ROI.

ROI is in the eye of the beholder

This focus on ROI or productivity has not been lost on the sellers of technology and services. For instance, research firm META Group uses "Return on Intelligence" as its moniker. The group has been promulgating the message of smart management and deployment of IT assets. ROI calculators abound on the web sites of many technology sellers. In fact, one specialty firm—Alinean in Orlando, FL— was formed in 2001 to help technology companies build ROI metrics and proof points for their products. IT productivity expert Paul Strassmann is on the board of directors; and Alinean Chairman Thomas Pisello recently wrote the book *IT Value Chain Management—Maximizing the ROI from IT Investments,* which discusses how to maximize ROI when IT is used to support business goals.

While tools such as these may appear to be a panacea, they have one significant problem: Nearly any technology can be shown to deliver ROI. A key challenge for technology sellers today is that there are too many products and too many ways to deliver ROI-based benefits on the market. Every IT vendor ranging from voice-activated e-mail to wireless connectivity to supply chain optimization is

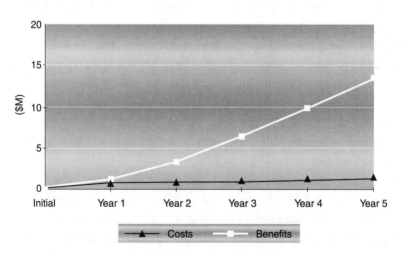

ROI calculators are being used by many technology vendors to justify their packages. The calculators, either internally developed or sold by companies such as Alinean, generate cost-benefit models to quantitatively show the benefits of certain types of software packages. The best use of these tools is to compare and analyze differing projects against each other within a single company.

putting ROI labels on its products, as illustrated on page 60. Benefits range from faster response times to better customer service to less inventory—the list goes on. Some of the benefits are quantitative (hard numbers like a 20 percent reduction in inventory) while others are qualitative (soft numbers such as a greater ability to sell more to existing customers). This new generation of calculators attempts to put a revenue generation or cost savings number on each type of benefit. These calculators have permitted every technology vendor to deliver an ROI story. Buyers now see a blur of ROI benefits with all potential sellers stating the same "buy now, save later" message.

As a result, the average CIO gets bombarded with these money-saving schemes. It is difficult for companies to decide which of them to choose. Which one out of a dozen potential IT projects makes the most sense for the business? In this case, an ROI tool may be useful in helping a buyer sift the best project from a dozen or more potential investments.

However, these tools should not be seen as a cure-all, because they have not increased the success rate of IT projects. The vast majority of buyers are still having a tough time showing positive results. ROI tools by themselves do not change the steps that companies must take to have a successful project—they merely help buyers understand the potential ROI. An ROI model has little to do with how well a technology is implemented by any given company. Until a more holistic view is taken in the selection and implementation of technology, ROI models will help companies better justify their purchases but not change the rates of project success or failure.

MOVING TOWARD IT-ENABLED PRODUCTIVITY

It will be a long time, if ever, before everyone agrees on the best mix of investments for IT. Productivity is highly debated among buyers and sellers of IT. These views range from irrelevance to a core measurement of economic health. One highly debated point is that productivity is calculated from the perspective of a standard workweek of 40 hours. Nowhere in the statistics is there any accounting for nonhourly employees who work in excess of the standard. This includes working overtime, at home, on weekends doing e-mail, and so forth. A workweek of 60-plus hours is typical for me and many of my peers. For many salaried workers, this has quietly become the norm. At the very least, this implies that productivity numbers are lower than stated by the federal government. Technology has allowed many people in the labor force to work longer hours, but not necessarily more productive ones.

Perhaps productivity and the impact of IT are being overthought, and a simpler view should be taken. Let's consider the definition of productivity gain: increasing the given output at a constant or declining cost. What happens to this definition when it's applied to IT? As the next figure shows, this train of thought implies that if IT really does lead to increases in productivity, then IT productivity gain can be measured in two ways: as a function of decreased IT cost for a set business benefit and as a function of increased business benefits with no additional technology spending.

If IT facilitates productivity gains, then every year, the IT cost ascribed to a given business function should decrease in price. The

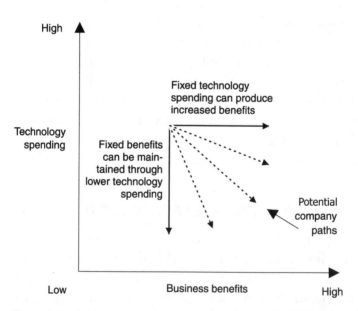

IT-based productivity. Companies can measure increased productivity from IT in two ways. One is through the reduction of IT costs for a simple unchanged business function year to year; the other is to increase the business benefits of any technology solution at a constant cost year to year. Companies will invest in a combination of the two.

cost to take an order, write an insurance policy, or check delivery status on a web site should decrease year to year. This is not a foreign or strange concept; it's what every company must do with its product lines to remain competitive.

When IT budgets are examined in this fashion, it changes the way in which spending is considered. These productivity gains should be a goal of every company, though few look at IT and productivity this way. IT groups, and those managing the IT budget, are in the best position to enable this type of reduction using a variety of asset-management techniques.

Another way to enhance IT productivity is to hold IT costs constant while increasing the business benefit derived from a deployed technology. In this case, different portions of already-installed technologies would be further exploited and used to increase revenue, decrease costs, increase customer satisfaction, or quicken delivery times. Every year, IT assets would be combed to see how a company could obtain more business benefits from what has already been purchased.

This productivity gain will come not from the IT group but from the business units. They must determine how to better utilize and derive benefits from an application that is already installed. Although this may sound difficult, many companies tap only the surface capabilities of their installed technology. Many executives would be amazed to see how many unused capabilities lie dormant in their technology assets.

Most companies will take a combination of these approaches and cut IT spending while using a step-function approach to increase the business value of what is installed. Companies will take a step or two down on their IT spending and then a step or two to the right to obtain enhanced benefits. Some cuts may be used to buy additional technology, which has its own set of business benefits.

These reductions might sound like a tall order, but they follow the same pattern of constant cost reductions that other highly competitive sectors follow. These include major original equipment manufacturers (OEMs) for automotive, electronics, retail, and other industries. Every year, these companies go into their planning cycles with the need to reduce the price of their products by a fixed percentage. The same can be done with IT. However, not many companies have chosen this way to manage and view their IT spending. If they did, better productivity numbers would be forthcoming.

Both buyers and sellers are trying to understand the real impact of technology and how best to use it and obtain business benefits. While sellers of technology emphatically state that IT delivers many benefits, some of the largest ones are taking no chances. In April 2003, MIT's Sloan School of Management formed the Information Work Productivity Council (IWPC). The IWPC's mission over the next three years is "to measure and improve the profitability of companies through the improvement of information-based work." More than $4.5 million in endowments has been pledged to the effort by such companies as Accenture, British Telecom, Cisco, Intel, Hewlett-Packard, SAP, Microsoft, and Xerox. The group also brings together many of the key economists and researchers who have investigated the relationship between productivity and IT.

Any skeptic worth his or her corrosive salt will question the pairing of the largest IT sellers in the world with the largest group of heretofore-independent economists. If the group can stay away from charged topics such as excessive market hype, aggressive sales forces/compensation plans, and inflated promises (and other seller-specific topics as a key contributor to IT inefficiencies), perhaps it can remain thoroughly independent.

SUR~~VIVAL~~ GUIDE
FOR BUYERS

PRODUCTIVITY
Here are a few steps that buyers can take to increase their IT productivity:

- **Create a business case for *every* type of technology purchase.** While some buyers may claim this cannot be done, it should be done for everything from a printer cord to a programming tool to a new accounting system. By forcing a real justification for a purchase rather than a statement like "We need more security," companies can quickly separate what is needed from what is not. Qualifiable benefits such as higher reliability and easier-to-customize solutions should be translated into business benefits, such as the ability to take more customer orders, fewer disruptions in deliveries, and quicker implementation of business strategies.

- **Do not following meaningless spending averages.** Spending averages show how much companies spend, not how well they use technology. Don't believe that you must spend more to be better than the competition. Look at industry averages with a careful eye to see what your competition is doing. Spending half as much may be the best strategy. The companies that are the best users of technology often spend much less than the industry average.

- **Be careful about how you use ROI calculations; create ongoing benchmarks.** ROI calculations are important, but make sure that they reflect the reality of how a technology will be rolled out and used. It is best to use ROI tools to evaluate a wide range of IT projects to understand which one delivers the highest value. Once a technology is rolled out, create a series of ongoing benchmarks (productivity, ROI, customer satisfaction, and others) to ensure that you are still obtaining value from your IT investment.

SURVIVAL GUIDE
FOR BUYERS

- **Have a strong business case or champion.** While it may sound unlikely, companies still go into technology projects without a focus on the business benefit derived from the technology deployed. Just because the IT group wants to deploy a promising technology doesn't mean that it will deliver any benefits to a corporation or its customers. New technologies such as wireless and instant messaging are cool, but without an identified and measurable business benefit, they will be a waste of corporate resources.

- **Segment large projects into smaller ones with hard milestones.** Large projects have high degrees of risk and should be carefully considered. Instead, projects should be deployed in a smaller, more metered way to control and manage problems and review benefits. If a three-year project no longer has a benefit one year in, because of a change in corporate direction, stop the project and cut your losses. Such a change should not be considered a failure but a success for a corporation that can spot and quickly react to changing business needs.

SURVIVAL GUIDE
FOR SELLERS

PRODUCTIVITY

Sellers should follow the previous steps as well, to ensure that their customers gain strong benefits from technology rather than just a bill. They can also:

- **Focus on customers/markets that can best benefit from the technology.** Technology companies do a relatively poor job of targeting and segmenting potential customers and markets. This makes many of them a mile wide and an inch deep in functional or technical offerings. Such companies need to hire more functional and business experts to better position and deploy their technologies for business benefit. The key to seller success is having a deep understanding of the problems and potentials for the industries you sell to.

- **Be willing to share in the risk.** In the current model for technology, the customer assumes all the risk with large up-front payments and the hope that the technology actually gets used as envisioned. Vendors should attempt to strike a better risk/reward relationship with customers to ensure that both sides profit from the partnership. By not being willing to take such a risk, sellers imply that their technologies will not deliver the ROI stated. Risk sharing implies a much more focused sales process, which targets not just the best prospects that will buy but also those that will succeed.

- **Promote products using rock-solid ROI examples from customers.** Buyers always like a good list of real-world examples to show how a product works for a real company. Don't be shy about getting your customers to help you promote the success they have had with your products. Without such proof points it will be hard to sell your products in an increasingly cynical market. In contract negotiations, include a clause that will permit you to reference each and every customer.

CHAPTER FIVE

TOO MUCH
OF A GOOD THING

"Since IT products are widely thought to have a three-year replacement cycle," goes the argument, "the replacement cycle is now overdue to kick in." I am quite dubious of the claim that there is a three-year shelf life for IT products. To me, this smacks of vendor-driven hype.

—Stephen Roach, chief economist,
Morgan Stanley[1]

Over a five-year period, we will be able to take out over 50 percent of our IT costs while significantly increasing total output.

—Toby Redshaw, corporate vice president,
Motorola's IT department

URING THE 1990S, it was good eating for those feasting at the corporate technology salad bar. Technology was easy to sell because so many companies were buying. Lots of application software buying meant lots of buying in related areas such as software tools and databases as well as server, PC, and storage hardware. An effort to get the best and fastest piece of equipment for anyone who wanted it fueled spending as never before. Because of this lack of discipline, few executives had any idea of how large their IT assets were, where they existed, or how they were being used. When companies started to evaluate their technology purchases, they were surprised to find out how much they had spent on IT.

"You wouldn't believe what we found once we started to look into our IT assets," said Tom, an IT manager for a multibillion-dollar electronics manufacturer. "We had no idea we had so much equipment."

Tom's company was typical. There was room upon room of unused IT equipment. Tom's company decided to inventory these systems. Besides finding that it had more technology than it thought, the company also found that some of the business units were using equipment that had been written off, taken off the network, and then put in storage to be disposed of as salvage.

This situation created both financial and legal problems for the company, but that wasn't the worst of it. "I don't even want to tell you how many systems we have that we are paying for that are not being used by anyone," lamented Tom.

Today, corporations have realized it's cleanup time. This was bluntly noted in a 2001 study by the Boston Consulting Group:[2] "Last year, the top 20 clients of the Boston Consulting Group devoted an average of $800 million to IT, or five to eight percent of their total expenditures. ...[M]uch is wasted as a result of several critical dysfunctions that plague IT organization and management of most companies."

Companies have started to address such problems with a renewed focus on cost control and spending restraint. A few new technology products aimed at helping companies better manage their IT assets have become available.

OVERBUYING IT

The past decade has seen huge increases in technology expenditures. According to statistics from the U.S. Department of Commerce, corporations purchased more than $3 trillion of IT-related capital equipment over the past decade. This led to an installed base of IT capital of more than $1 trillion by 1999 and translated to a cumulative investment estimated between $8,000 and $10,000 per employee.[3] Today, this investment per employee is much larger given the fact that private employment in the United States was approximately the same in 2003 as it was in 1999 and that companies spent more than $1.6 trillion on IT capital investments in the years 2000 through 2003.[4] As the figure below shows, the majority of investment was in software.

At the time, many companies believed that it was prudent to plan for growth and overcapacity. Such companies spent much of the 1990s deploying and integrating complex technologies at a rapid pace. This pace overshadowed strict spending controls. Few companies or management teams sought strict accounting from their IT groups. A booming economy and rapidly changing technology fostered an environment that quickened rather than slowed corporate adoption of new technologies. All of this led to overspending in three principal ways:

- Paying more for technology and services than appropriate for the business benefit garnered

- Purchasing more software technology than would be used (shelfware)

- Purchasing more hardware technology than needed (overcapacity)

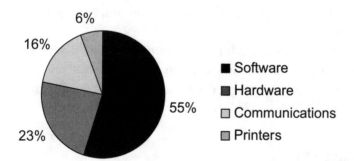

IT capital stock per employee. In 1999, each company had an installed base of technology per employee of $8,100. The vast majority of this investment was in software both for personal productivity and corporate automation. Much of this buildup occurred in the late 1990s much faster than the growth of the previous 20 years. *Source: BEA, McKinsey Global Institute.*

The price of technology

The past practices of overspending have become much more apparent to executives today as technology bills and budgets are being scrutinized. This close examination has forced companies to realize that value and IT pricing are hard to correlate. When sellers price their software, they often focus more on what it costs to build and sell it than what it is actually worth to a buyer. For example, one Silicon Valley software client hired me in 2002 to help formulate its product pricing. This client offered an infrastructure technology that was not well understood by the average buyer. Based on its venture-capital expectations, costs, and corporate goals, the company thought that an initial price of $250,000 for the software was appropriate.

Yet it wasn't clear what a buyer would be getting. The client had little product literature, no standard lists of features or functions, no references, and a limited roadmap of what would be built in the future. The client still believed that the product was worth $250,000. But would anyone pay that much? Not likely.

The trouble for the client was that the product was very new, with fewer than 40 years of development effort behind it. It was also not finished; the software had many functional holes and was unstable. Few buyers were going to make a large commitment to this type of product. The best path for the client was to give away the product early on and obtain valuable feedback from buyers. This feedback could then be used to build a product that would meet the needs of a target market. When presented with this idea, the client replied coldly, "That's not in our business plan. You need to come up with a better idea than that." In the middle of 2003, the company was barely getting by. It never got the $250,000 from any customer.

This view has been common to many sellers of technology: Charge a lot of money up front for an interesting idea, and get the buyer to co-fund the research and development (R&D) investment. This strategy will not work in the future.

"Customer-funded R&D is going away," according to Bill Janeway, vice chairman of Warburg Pincus, a leading venture-capital company. Janeway is right. Buyers have become much more savvy about putting millions of dollars on the table before a single piece of code is delivered, although companies continue to make errors in judgment about how much technology they should buy in advance.

This is one of the many problems that the state of California had in 2001 when it signed a long-term statewide contract with Oracle for technology products and services worth $95 million. When the contract was examined by an independent auditor, the auditor found that instead of saving the state more than $100 million as Oracle claimed would happen with the consolidation of multiple contracts, it was costing the state an additional $40 million.[5]

It didn't help public relations that Oracle had made substantial contributions to the reelection funds of former governor Gray Davis and other state officials. It was probably nothing more than an aggressive sales force taking advantage of an inexperienced state procurement group.

"General Services' negotiating team was inexperienced and unprepared, with no expertise in software contracts and no in-depth knowledge of Oracle's business and contracting practices," the audit report found. "In short, the state had never before negotiated [a licensing agreement] and let Oracle and its reseller, Logicon, use common vendor negotiating tactics to push through a largely one-sided contract."[6] This transaction was a very public reminder of the increasingly expensive and risky path taken by companies making large technology purchases.

An expensive no-brainer

Inattention to price was a common theme in the 1990s. Once a company started down this path, it was hard (and sometimes politically risky) to pull back. For example, Will, the CIO of a Fortune 100 company, had decided to purchase 10,000 user licenses from SAP. At the time, SAP had a complex but flexible pricing scheme that had over a half-dozen user types (full use, development, departmental, customer, and others) and a sliding scale of per-user pricing ranging from hundreds to thousands of dollars depending on the type of user. For Will, this didn't work.

"There is no way that I can figure out how our company is going to use this stuff," he said. "I'm just going to buy 10,000 full-use licenses and let it go."

Will could have saved at least $5 million if he had spent time determining how company employees would use SAP. A back-of-the-envelope estimate could have easily cut $1 million from his software invoice. But Will had little desire to make such a change, for two reasons. The first was that he was fearful of needing additional licenses (unbudgeted costs) in the future. Second, he didn't want to inform the board of directors that initial estimates on the project were high. It was easier to play it safe and spend the extra $5 million.

Bloated software inventories

Buying excess capacity in software because of the inability to accurately forecast or plan for demand is extremely common. When companies buy a large suite of applications with many user licenses, typically only a few of each are used. But it gets worse. After using only, say, 10 out of 100 licenses of a package they purchased less than a year before, clients often came back looking to buy yet another software package. This lack of use has shown up in a variety of surveys. For example:

- Morgan Stanley gave shelfware (e.g., software licenses that were not being used) as the key reason for a slowdown in software spending between 2000 and 2002. In a 2002 Morgan Stanley survey published in *CFO* magazine, out of 300 CIOs "one-third said they had unused database licenses, 12 percent said they had unused consumer relationship management (CRM) licenses, 20 percent reported unused enterprise resources planning (ERP) licenses, and just over 10 percent reported unused supply chain management (SCM) licenses."[7]

- A 2003 Gartner, Inc. survey revealed that more than 40 percent of the CRM software licenses bought by businesses go unused. "Buying more software licenses than needed may seem like a wise investment in the short term, but over time it costs more," said Beth Eisenfeld, research director for Gartner.[8]

- In a 2001 AMR Research poll of companies that purchased supply chain software, 85 percent of all buyers were using only one or two modules. An updated 2003 report indicated that many buyers have spent the last few years implementing what they purchased two or three years earlier.[9]

Such buying burdens companies with excess payments on both a one-time (initial license fee) and continuing basis (long-term maintenance). The effect of these overpayments is a mushrooming of expenses and costs. Each project that represents an excess adds more inefficiencies to the IT budget. The IT budget then becomes filled with waste and consequently much less efficient. The maintenance budget, which gives buyers upgrades and varying degrees of support for the systems they buy, is one of the largest areas of waste.

Maintenance: the 28 percent solution

In the late 1990s, a client was looking for advice after he had stopped paying maintenance on a software package. "I went off maintenance for BPCS [an ERP product sold by System Software Associates] three years ago when I didn't realize that Y2K was going to be an issue. I need to get SSA's Y2K fix, but they won't give it to me unless I renew my maintenance contract," Tony said.

Buyers of technology spend a lot of time negotiating initial software license fees without realizing downstream maintenance costs. Maintenance payments to sellers represent much more than the initial license fee over the lifetime of the license. These fees are high-margin "cash cows" that sellers protect and bargain hard for, particularly when a customer has stopped buying new licenses—even more so when they have stopped paying for maintenance.

"Let me guess, Tony. They want to charge you for the last three years plus a penalty, right?"

"Yeah, it almost comes to as much as I initially spent on the package six years ago. What should I do?"

"Your options are not really good at this point. It's too late to buy something new. You either have to pay up or try to patch something together using a combination of techniques that our software tools folks [at Gartner] could talk to you about. What do you want to do?"

"Transfer me over to your tools people."

He didn't like any of the options given to him by the tools people—options that included rewriting large portions of the software or turning back the clock on the software. He was compromised because he wasn't sure of his legal rights concerning the software. In the end, he wound up paying SSA the money it had initially demanded.

Vinnie Mirchandani, CEO of the JetStream Group, a consultancy that helps companies maximize their software and service investments, believes that many companies are greatly overpaying for maintenance. "Some users are paying 28 percent [of list price] at Oracle, and they really don't need it," he said. "Maintenance includes telephone support, bug fixes, and new releases, but some buyers don't really need all of that."

Competition is changing the market for maintenance. For example, in the mid 1990s, gray-market providers emerged to service legacy software packages from Dun & Bradstreet (eventually acquired by Geac) and others at a large discount. Such alternatives continue to challenge a somewhat inefficient market. "There are very few industries in the world where the OEM requires you to go back for support. It's almost antitrust," according to Mirchandani.

This new competition will ultimately be good for buyers.

Most companies do not realize that maintenance payments are typically based on the list price of the software's license fees. When software is purchased, these license fees are often heavily discounted. So when buyers purchase software at a 50 percent discount, they often end up making maintenance payments of 40 percent or more every year thereafter on the price they initially paid.

Through more aggressive procurement policies and the expectation of maintenance discounts, users have started to better manage these costs. They are seeking—and getting—concessions from sellers to minimize long-term software maintenance costs.

LESSONS LEARNED

These types of expenditures, plus the long delay between buying technology and seeing benefits, is changing the way companies are purchasing IT. As buyers lick their wounds over aborted projects and review their inventories, few are stepping up to the plate for large expenditures. Average selling prices for software are down and aren't expected to come back up.

"We used to be able to get high six and low seven figure deals easily, a few years ago. No one would really evaluate the cost. It was great," said one CEO of a supply chain vendor. "Now customers are buying much more incrementally."

Such vendors have only themselves to blame, as the experience of semiconductor manufacturer Applied Materials proves. In 2001, Applied Materials invested more than $80 million in a supply chain project with i2 Technologies that was difficult to launch. "Vendors were licking their chops when they saw us," said Mike Kalmar, a supply chain manager for Applied Materials.

A $60 million extension to the project was slated to be launched in 2002, but Applied Materials started to review the cost and benefits of the extension. The company soon determined that i2 Technologies' initial proposal was excessive and decided to stop the extension and regroup its efforts.

Applied Materials learned an important lesson from this and is looking at all IT spending now through a very different lens. "We are looking at IT spending in a much more metered way," Kalmar said. "Even when the economy comes back, watching our IT costs will still be a focus for the company."

Corporations are no longer interested in the "big-bang, big-buck" endeavors and are forcing IT groups to pursue smaller initial investments. One such trend is the movement by some companies toward a pay-as-you-go or subscription-based license model. (See chapter 11 for more information on this trend.) Another outgrowth is short-term ROI.

A recent poll of enterprise software executives indicated that more than 75 percent of them believe that customers are expecting a positive ROI in less than one year after purchasing the software.[10] For buyers, this expectation represents a big change. Purchasing and implementing IT projects incrementally minimizes the risk of failure and gives companies a better view as to what will work within their business. It will also help them minimize future spending on more technology than they will use. For sellers, this is a hard value to deliver because it often takes at least three to six months to install such software, which leaves a very small window for benefits to be derived. Perhaps the IT industry needs to take a cue from others.

ASSET MANAGEMENT: USING WHAT YOU HAVE

In the United States, power companies typically maintain anywhere from 15 to 30 percent excess capacity beyond their peak loads to ensure continuous service to their customers, as the figure below shows. IT shops work in the same fashion as they supply computing resources to their customers. Like their power-plant brethren, they need to ensure that there is always enough excess network, storage, memory, computing, and capacity within the system so that business processes can always flow smoothly and quickly.

However, unlike their power-plant counterparts, IT shops traditionally have not managed their capacity anywhere near this 15 to 30 percent range. Instead, they run at a vast overcapacity, in some areas upward of 90 percent. Part of this overcapacity is due to the high degree of complexity of IT and the variety of connected and associated systems that must be dynamically balanced to ensure good performance. Even the best intentions, however, have not gone unpunished. Compare how many times your power goes out versus how many times your computing resources go out. The ratio will not be a favorable one.

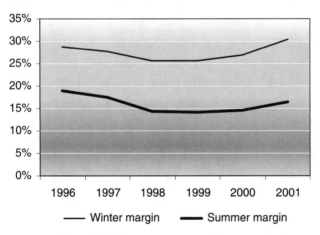

U.S. electric capacity reserve, 1996–2001.[11] IT departments function in the same way a utility company generates electricity. They must have an excess of capacity to handle peak loads; they have traditionally overbought capacity to ensure satisfactory performance. IT groups are starting to better manage capacity and cut their reserves to emulate the levels of U.S. power companies. *Source: U.S. Department of Energy.*

Delivering good computing performance at a reasonable cost is not a challenge because companies have purchased too little, but rather because of the inability to manage and segment application, communications, storage, and other loads, particularly on Unix and Windows equipment. Such was not the problem 20 or more years ago with mainframe technology because it came with software that managed application loads efficiently.

Managing the assets (both software and hardware) of an IT portfolio is one of many old, timeworn rabbits consultants pull out of their hats when clients ask for help. Buyers will need to swallow this and other medicinal remedies to help their IT groups return to optimum operational health. Few companies, however, have taken full advantage of how these techniques can help them.

Systems management: getting more out of assets

The recognition of the need for asset management is fueling a large growth market in IT called *systems management*. This market helps buyers better manage their systems performance. Basically, it helps companies use their existing systems and assets more efficiently. It is not a word processing program or accounting system, yet it is just as essential to most companies, given the wide array of applications they support as well as technologies that they use. Without such software, it is difficult to gauge and manage the performance of any corporate IT system.

Performance is difficult to determine unless it stares you right in the face. In a factory, it is simple to view machines at work. At a restaurant, cooks are preparing food diligently and quickly. Computing is much different. A room full of computers working at maximum capacity looks the same as computers that are idling unless you have a tool, as utility companies do, to examine and understand the usage and load on the system.

John is a longtime client of mine who works in the chemical industry. He did an excellent job installing his fairly complex and under-budget SAP solution. But a few years ago, he developed a problem.

John was running the U.S. and European parts of his business out of two service centers located in the United States. Without warning, user response times and performance dropped dramatically. He couldn't figure out what had gone wrong.

"I was knocking myself out over it, when I talked to some folks in our European Group," he explained. "I found out that they were kicking off a big batch run right when our customer service group was getting the highest number of calls. We just changed the time of the run, and now everything is fine."

John's problem seemed simple after it was discovered, but the difficulty he had identifying it was due to a lack of visibility within his large and complex system. He needed what is increasingly being sold by vendors—systems management for all the different parts of an IT operation. To become more efficient with the use of IT, companies, like the utility industries with large control rooms, must create their own set of management controls. As systems become more distributed, these capabilities have become essential. Some of the largest and fastest-growing software vendors today are in this space.

"It's not real hard to show value with our application," said Gary Bloom, CEO of Veritas, a major seller of storage management software. "It's not a hard sell. We just go in and tell clients how they can cut back [on their storage equipment] and save money."

**Systems management:
keeping resources in check**
Systems management software has been in existence nearly as long as computers have been around. This type of software attempts to efficiently match the availability of resources (e.g., hardware processing, network, storage) with the need to ensure good performance and service. (Other types of systems management applications assist IT managers in starting up, shutting down, and maintaining their equipment efficiently.) In some organizations, as little as 10 percent of all available resources are used at any single moment, making systems management software very valuable for the potential resources it can make available. Such software has become more important over the past decade as applications and IT resources have become much more physically distributed within organizations. All large corporations use varying degrees of this type of software to manage their operations. It is offered by companies such as IBM, Computer Associates, Veritas Software, and EMC. Marc Andreessen, the founder of Netscape, has started Opsware, Inc., which sells software to automate IT operations.

This approach has not been lost on new vendors, such as Palo Alto, CA–based VMware, which is taking mainframe-systems management techniques to market. (In December 2003, EMC purchased VMware for $635 million in cash.) The ease of initial purchase and proliferation of web-based and other applications has facilitated an undisciplined array of equipment in many companies. Companies have added large numbers of Intel-based computer servers, but they have not supplemented such servers with systems management technology to optimize their use. VMware, by imparting the same type of clustering and management approach that proprietary mainframes use, has been able to decrease the total cost of ownership for companies using Intel-based computing by one third to two thirds.

"We have seen the [computing] utilization of some customers go from 5 to 80 percent," said Diane Greene, president and CEO of VMware. "Most companies have no idea how much capacity they really are wasting." These gains, in effect, let companies cut 70 percent or more of their computing power. "Many companies have a difficult time believing that they can cut this much computing power from their IT centers," according to Greene.

Jason Martin, director of professional services for VMware, said that this point was brought home recently with a new client that was using Windows NT extensively.

"The client was using 75 computers running [Microsoft's] NT [operating system] that were on average three years old. They had built a lot of custom software that was deployed on different processors ... they felt that they could not touch or change anything even though they believed that they could get more efficiency from consolidating," said Martin. "We were able to help them take the number of computers down to three, and they probably could have gotten away with one."

This type of consolidation saved the client a great deal of money devoted not only to hardware but also to the labor associated with management of the 75 systems. Having a smaller number of systems enabled the client to drop the number of staffers dedicated to managing the systems, and maintenance charges on hardware are lower due to a smaller number of systems. These results are leading the client to adopt VMware for another project that will consolidate a large data center containing more than 400 computing servers.

What you don't know can cost you

Although many systems management products are helping companies better manage what they know they have, a huge number of systems within companies are unknown. Traditional inventory techniques have been used to find them, but there are always pockets (sometimes quite large) of undocumented and undiscovered technologies. A few new companies, such as BDNA (Mountain View, CA), are attempting to capitalize on this issue.

Since 2000, BDNA has been quietly building technology that can be hooked to any communications network and automatically detect all the devices and software that reside on the network, regardless of type. It detects all systems, both known and unknown. This is a capability that typical systems management software never had before—a view of all assets, as the figure on the next page shows. By mid-2003, BDNA had scanned the IT assets of more than 20 companies and was implementing its technology at over half a dozen corporations.

"One of the biggest things we have found is that companies have no idea of the number of active Internet Protocol [IP] nodes that exist in their corporations," said Constantin Delivanis, CEO and founder of BDNA. "Less than 10 percent of all listed nodes are active and used." This means that the scanned companies have many more communications routers [a type of hardware to manage network traffic] than are needed.

"Companies also are underestimating the amount of Linux servers that exist in their companies. They are off by a factor of 10," he added. "And application and database software? That's a whole other business." Motorola is one company that is beginning to harvest a great deal of savings in this area.

Motorola's journey to IT productivity

Motorola is one of the early adopters of BDNA software. It started to use the BDNA product while it was in the middle of an IT rationalization exercise. "In 2001, Motorola made the decision to

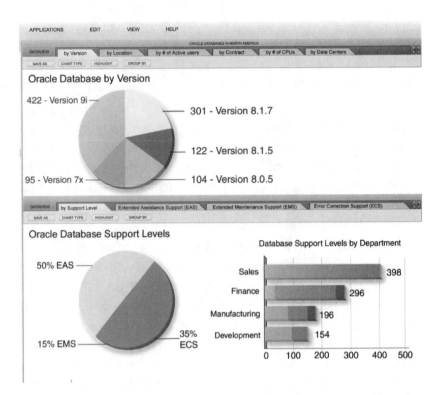

BDNA can help companies better understand the type of assets in use. The upper graph in this figure shows the number of different Oracle versions that are currently used by a corporation. The bottom figure supplements this information by showing the different levels of support for the database by department throughout the corporation. *Source: BDNA*

streamline its IT efforts throughout each Motorola business," according to Toby Redshaw, a corporate vice president for IT at Motorola. "For example, we were using Oracle as a single approach for ERP and all but one business had deployed it (Motorola's semi-conductor unit uses SAP). Unfortunately, they had all acted independently and differently. As a result, we had several different instances of Oracle sitting on different [hardware] platforms, which is a very inefficient use of resources."

The cost of these differences has been significant to Motorola. For example, one of its smaller business units did a simple installation of Oracle, which cost nearly $13 million. By consolidating cross-sector efforts, Motorola was able to save millions of dollars each year. Key to this savings was a team at Motorola that compiled the most elemental facts and figures about how much technology Motorola owned. The findings surprised senior management because "most people have no idea how much gets spent in this area," said Redshaw.

Attacking IT costs

A few years ago, Motorola started a two-pronged attack on IT costs: Fusion and Alliance. Fusion was a program to consolidate and optimize Motorola's use of hardware. Alliance is doing the same for software. "[In the early 2000s] each business was doing their own thing and buying whatever they wanted," said Redshaw. "When somebody wanted a box, we bought them a box. When we finally looked at what we created, we had over 150 data centers of varying sizes around the world."

Motorola put together a team to count and measure the systems that were in place. By the end of 2002, Motorola was able to reduce its spending in hardware by more than $100 million, not counting reductions in yearly maintenance contracts. Software was a different matter.

You can't see software or know how it's being used or how many people are using it. If properly managed, it is a great opportunity for most companies to save money. As mentioned earlier, traditional systems management tools from vendors such as IBM, Hewlett-Packard, and Computer Associates help speed the performance of systems and do rudimentary tracking; they do not tell you about the nature of use or license structures. BDNA is helping Motorola discover what it does not know about what it has bought or inherited via merger/acquisition, and what it is using.

"We first targeted Oracle [with BDNA] because we are a big customer," said Redshaw. "We found significant overspending and underutilization. With this information, we can renegotiate our contract for a large cost savings." Motorola gathered detailed user-level utilization and history data for Oracle at Motorola. This knowledge permitted the company to obtain significant savings.

Motorola also decided to determine how pervasive Linux was within the corporation. The BDNA tool told Motorola the number was close to 10 percent of its computing resources. "When we get to the next level of analysis, I think we will find somewhere between 600 and 800 Linux servers within the company," said Redshaw.

This initial (and continuing) examination of its global IT resources has made Motorola rethink how it spends money on IT. When it first calculated its spending on IT using the conventional measure of spending as a percentage of sales, it came up with a number somewhere between 4 and 5 percent. It expects to cut that in half over the next few years.

Motorola is taking a path that many companies will need to travel in the future. As a former Motorola CIO put it, the direction is simple: "Clean up, catch up, beat up." Motorola finished its cleanup phase and is now positioned to execute the other two areas of an integrated IT and business strategy: catch up to and beat its competition. So far, Motorola has been clear and focused.

As shown in the figure below, Motorola's IT group spent a great deal of money in the 1990s and delivered business benefits that were proportionally lower than the dollars spent on them. The limited benefits were due to redundant (and sometimes conflicted) business systems, excessive hardware and software resources, and inattention

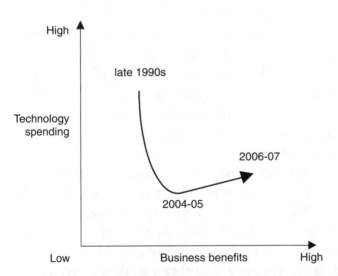

Motorola's path of IT spending from the late 1990s to the future. Motorola has spent over three years slashing its IT cost structure and understanding how to best use technology. It is now on a path to take these reduced and optimized resources and deliver much higher business benefits.

to IT budgeting. After focusing on its IT assets and how they affected business, Motorola has been able to cut its IT budgets while getting the same (or slightly more) business benefits from technology dollars.

THE PATH TO ENLIGHTENMENT

Unfortunately, this type of hard medicine (asset management) taken by Motorola and others is not something that many companies will adopt quickly. According to Gartner, only a few companies have truly enlightened views on asset management; most hover between a chaotic and a reactive style. I believe that this will change. Over the next four years, financial pressures will force IT groups to either shape up or ship out in terms of asset management, as the next figure illustrates. The more intelligent and resourceful IT managers will survive and thrive in a more streamlined environment down the road.

"Excessive spending in the 1990s, the economic downturn, and declining margins in our business are forcing us to focus on the cost

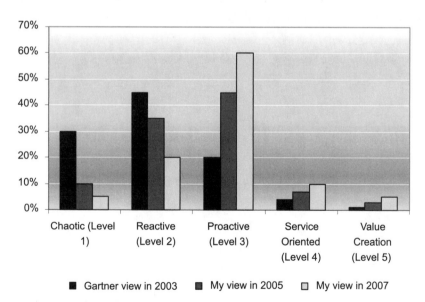

Information technology asset management styles. Asset management is a discipline that most IT shops practice poorly. Over the next two to four years, management pressure will cause the vast majority of companies to become much more proactive in their approach to asset management.[12] *Source: Gartner Inc. and Wapiti LLC*

of IT," said Diane, a vice president of supply chain operations for an electronics manufacturer. "We have too many underutilized systems and expensive software licenses. That is going to change."

Eliminating excessive IT spending requires a few things. First, many groups need to recognize that the decentralization of the 1980s combined with the technology hype of the 1990s facilitated sloppy procurement practices and lax management. These practices and management capabilities need to be supplanted with clear operational goals and metrics. Effective use of IT is all about good business; it is not about cool technology.

A provocative article titled "IT Doesn't Matter" by Nicholas Carr appeared in the May 2003 issue of the *Harvard Business Review*. The article received a lot of attention. Its point—that IT is unimportant or undifferentiating—misstates the challenge for most companies. At the end of the day, technology must be deployed in the least expensive, most efficient way possible regardless of the type of technology used. The days of youthful indulgence are over, and expensive experimentation must give way to a goal-oriented focus and execution. The days of strong benefits are ahead at much lower costs, with IT systems that will be simpler to manage and operate.

SURVIVAL GUIDE
FOR BUYERS

DOWNSIZING IT DEPARTMENTS

Dramatically lowering IT costs will be an unpleasant but necessary exercise for companies over the next few years. Here are a few steps companies should take to downsize IT departments:

- **Inventory IT assets.** If you don't know what you have, then you can't think about the problem. Manual processes that combine IT and business unit teams designed to discover what a company has—and what it needs—will be key. Automated tools such as those offered by BDNA will ferret out hidden and underutilized assets. Don't be afraid to reexamine the initial business case and use assumptions of technology purchases. If they are too expensive, plan to swap out for less expensive systems.

- **Write off waste.** It may be hard, but you must write off large unused IT investments that remain on the books because no one wants to take the blame. Be honest about what is used, and just do it. Underutilized assets warp the economics of IT and hurt the funding of new initiatives. Don't search for someone to blame, but instead look at the lessons learned through bad investments.

- **Manage assets.** While a new server from Dell may appear inexpensive, when you buy 400 of them and need a crew of professionals to manage them, the costs add up. Be ruthless when consolidating hardware. Most companies are utilizing a very small percentage of processing, storage, and networking assets. Service, license, maintenance, and labor savings will follow.

- **Review maintenance and service contracts.** Companies leave a lot of money on the table by not reviewing their IT contracts on an annual basis. Some companies pay over 40 percent of the net price paid for software and hardware annually. Contracts are often signed at initial purchase, put in a drawer, and paid on an annual basis without

SURVIVAL GUIDE
FOR BUYERS

much thought. These contacts must be taken out of that drawer, dusted off, examined for savings, and then renegotiated. Seek credits from vendors whose products are not being used fully.

SURVIVAL GUIDE
FOR SELLERS

DEALING WITH DOWNSIZED CUSTOMERS
As buyers cut back, sellers will be faced with revenue shortfalls in areas that they considered cash cows. Sellers can do a few things to cope with the potential revenue fallout:

- **Be proactive with clients.** Don't wait for customers to throw you out because they have underutilized your technology. Get your sales force to better work with your current customers to understand what products are best (as well as worst) used. Approach them with how to best receive value from their current investments. If their systems are underutilized, help them increase their use, or be flexible in renegotiating service and maintenance contracts.

- **Look for new opportunities and cracks in the competition.** If an incumbent vendor is showing little value, use that opportunity to help the customer save money and receive better service. Help clients understand the value (or lack thereof) in competitive solutions, and then tell them how you will make them more efficient and better solve their business needs. It may not be the big sale you'd hoped for, but by helping the client, you pave the way for future successes.

- **Review sales and go-to-market strategies.** Successful companies in the future will not be those that oversell and overpromise to customers but those that show value on a continuing basis. Subscription-based revenue models somewhat force this hand. (See chapter 11 for more on this topic.) Sales and marketing plans need to be altered to ensure that a successful sale is followed by a successful implementation that delivers the expected business benefits. The traditional "hunter" type salesperson needs to be replaced and/or supplemented with a more consultative "gatherer" sales professional who will look to continue to increase the use and value of a technology within his or her client base.

CHAPTER SIX

BUSINESS —
LEAN AND SIMPLE

Anything that can affect industries whose total revenue base is many hundreds of billions of dollars is a big deal.
—Andrew Grove, CEO, Intel Corp.[1]

Under NO circumstances lose against Linux.
—Orlando Ayala, senior vice president, Microsoft[2]

O NE OF THE IRONIES OF IT is that after more than 20 years of trying to get away from centralized computing technology, the Internet has brought us all back to that point once again. Like clothing fashions, IT approaches that were all but discarded a decade ago are now back in style. But unlike those cheesy fashions of the 1960s and '70s, this centralized style of computing is likely to stay around. During a talk I presented a few years ago on integration and the changing nature of computer deployments, this point was brought home to me.

"So when you get down to it, we are really going back to the era of host-based, green-screen computing," I said. A young man sitting in the back of the room raised his hand.

"What is a green screen?" Others in the audience nodded their heads; they too were interested in an answer. Feeling as old as the hills, I realized that an entire generation of workers has emerged knowing nothing but PCs and graphical user interfaces (GUIs). To communicate a basic understanding of something I mistakenly thought was common knowledge, a bit of history was needed.

"It's the name given to computer terminals at the time [before PCs] because their screens were green," I explained. "These were truly dumb devices; all they did was display alphanumeric images that were sent to them via a centralized computer. For example, many PC-based checkout registers at stores still display information using just alphanumeric characters.

"The important processing for most of the applications that run over the Web is occurring at a remote site, just as it did in the 1960s and '70s with mainframes and minicomputers. So when you use the Internet extensively, the PC becomes a fairly expensive, idling dumb terminal. There is no fundamental difference."

In an attempt to simplify the way they deploy computing resources, companies have started to enthusiastically embrace a style of computing that is 40 years old. The minicomputer, PC, and client-server technologies of the 1980s and '90s were supposed to reduce computing costs, but their complexity and distribution actually increased it. In the late 1990s, companies added application and web servers to take advantage of the Internet. Today, they are looking for a simpler, more standard way to deploy IT.

Simplicity will mean different things to different companies. To some, it will mean consolidating their technology choices to fewer companies; to others it will mean implementing "just good enough" or "80-percent" solutions to meet business challenges. For still others, simplicity will translate to low-cost, widely deployed technology solutions. This change will come once IT budget managers realize that the difficulties of using new and different technology have been underemphasized while the rewards have been oversold.

CREATING STANDARDS

The global move toward IT simplicity will start with creating global standards. To understand the potential benefits we can gain from standardizing IT interfaces and approaches, we need only look at the industrial benefits gained by the standardization of time, just over a century ago.

Midday, traditionally defined as the moment in the day when the sun is at its highest point in the sky, was a simple and precise standard for time used throughout history—that is, until a new technology (trains) replaced an old one (horse and oxen) in the transportation business. Since the sun reaches the highest point at different times in locations with different longitudes, the traditional midday depended on geographic location. Any two points with longitudes differing by a degree had clocks off by four minutes. By the 1880s, trains were traversing many degrees of longitude in short, predictable periods. So when it was noon in Chicago, it was 11:50 A.M. in St. Louis and 12:18 P.M. in Detroit. This made it hard for businesses—particularly the railroads, which traversed time zones—to operate in an efficient manner.

These issues led to a great innovation: the creation of standard time in 1883. Railroad companies standardized time around four time zones in the United States, which continues to this day. Business, and life in general, became easier.

Today, as companies winnow down their technology investments, they too are looking for their version of standard time. Their pursuit of technological standards has taken many paths. A decade ago, Internet protocols were the new standard time. Other standards include PC hardware, Structured Query Language (SQL) for databases, Ethernet for networking, and COBOL for programming. Every decade has seen numerous standards and specifications created for myriad areas of IT.

These standards, however, have commingled into a Gordian Knot of messy, expensive, and complex computer systems. It wasn't a conscious decision to create this tangle; initiative after initiative was built to address a specific problem and then thrown into an IT drawer. When companies look to reverse this challenge, they often turn to standards, either de facto or de jour, to decrease their costs and increase their IT productivity.

Fine-tuning information technology

It may sound odd that the Web will become a corporate cost savior given all of the excessive spending that appeared in the late 1990s, but it will. Today, companies are using strategically placed web-based tools and applications to extend their investments. Lessons corporations have learned via Internet deployment include the following:

- **Simpler is better.** The history of technology indicates that once people and companies discover how to deploy technologies easily and cost-effectively, the technologies proliferate. The IT community is on the verge of realizing significant cost reductions in hardware, software, and labor through simplification. Deployment of centralized Internet architectures will be key to realizing this goal.

- *New* **does not necessarily mean** *improved.* Many companies continue to effectively run their corporations on 20-year-old COBOL systems. IBM believes that over 70 percent of all the world's transactions are still being run on such systems.[3] Vendors of packaged software want customers to upgrade their solutions on at least a biannual basis. In many cases, such changes are not in the best interest of the business. Coexistence between existing and new technology is key to corporate IT productivity and effectiveness.

The Web is facilitating myriad new applications. More important, it is providing a new structure and mechanism to decrease IT costs within corporations. Opportunities for IT cost reduction via the Web include:

- Using the Internet as a communications mechanism to facilitate inexpensive and simple communications between people and programs (a step already taken by most companies)

- Using Internet-based mainframe-like architectures to decrease cost and complexity through centralization of resources

- Reusing and integrating freeware and inexpensive software via a variety of web services, decreasing the cost of developing, modifying, and integrating technology

These points are not wasted on companies that devote a large portion of their IT resources to integrating different technology platforms.

Integration via the Web

One of the largest technology expenses any company must support is integration of application processes and data. Custom programming, which accounts for two-thirds of all capitalized spending on software, is yet another big bucket. The table below ranks the various IT spending categories.

Internet protocols, many of which were introduced in the early 1990s, are the fundamental standard that allows users on the Internet to access other web sites. Web services permit a more significant level of access and integration than Internet protocols and represent a collection of technologies that provide an additional baseline of standardization. Using web services, computers can access applications and data that exist on the Web without human intervention. While this sounds promising, there is a catch.

The history of technology standards and specifications has proven to be problematic, with many standards never gaining widespread use. Web services may turn out differently because of their focus on simplifying and lowering the cost and complexity of computing.

As the diagram on the next page shows, many companies still have an untidy array of technologies and approaches for integrating processes and data. Web services offer companies the hope of solving

The top 10 IT spending priorities in 2002–03. CFOs and CIOs are well aligned with spending priorities. Application integration consumes a significant portion of IT budgets and is one of the highest budget priorities.[4] *Source: Saugatuck Technology and CFO Publishing.*

Top 10 spending priorities in 2002–03 (ranking [% respondents])	CFOs	CIOs
Security software	1 (45%)	4-tied (32%)
Application integration	2 (36%)	2 (34%)
Website enhancement	3 (31%)	1 (39%)
Windows 2000/XP upgrades (server)	4 (30%)	8 (27%)
CRM software	5 (28%)	4-tied (32%)
Windows 2000/XP upgrades (desktop)	6 (27%)	6-tied (29%)
ERP software/ERP upgrades	7-tied (25%)	10-tied (24%)
Data-mining	7-tied (25%)	10-tied (24%)
E-commerce initiatives	7-tied (25%)	3 (33%)
Custom development	10 (22%)	6-tied (29%)

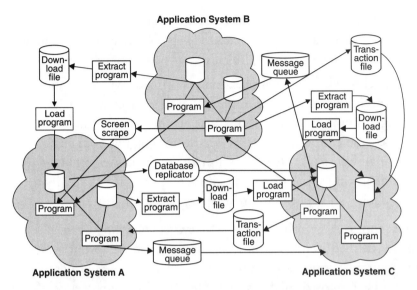

Application System B

Typical enterprise integration in a corporation. An ungainly web of complex and unwieldy integration technologies and points exists within many corporations, the result of decades of acquisitions and point approaches to integrate different types of technologies and business practices. Their cost and upkeep represent a significant drain on IT budgets. *Source: Gartner Inc.*

this problem cost-effectively because they approach integration from a different perspective. Web services[5] are software components that interact with each other across the Internet in a standardized way, allowing transactions to occur between various kinds of computers and systems. This means that any piece of software that uses web services can, given the right circumstances, integrate and communicate with another piece of software that uses web services. This implies the following:

- Integration is prebuilt into applications. Many applications are written as a chunk of code with little ability to link to or integrate with other chunks of code. (This obviously doesn't include such things as subroutines and application programming interfaces [APIs] where links for other chunks of code are necessarily specified.) Web service–based integration permits multiple applications or services to be integrated and combined.

- Pieces of software or services can be used to assemble an application. While many software tools have been created to improve productivity, the ability of companies to reuse or assemble applications from existing or purchased software has been limited. Software that uses web services can be assembled from different sources, literally anywhere on a network.

- Web service–based applications can run anywhere without modification. Because of the way web services approach programming and integration, once an application is written or assembled it can run on any platform, ranging from an IBM mainframe to a Dell PC. This reduces the cost of building and deploying applications and gives companies the flexibility to deploy an application on any platform at any time.

This approach is called a *service-based architecture.* Instead of a highly defined point interface or contact, a more abstract level of programming is used. Service-based architectures are not new. They were first proposed in the mid-1990s. With the emergence of the Web, companies have started to consider full-scale adoption of this approach. Together, these approaches and solutions create a simpler and more maintainable IT system.

Web services have a great potential to reduce the cost and complexity of IT. Early adopters have been successful with their projects when they've approached the use of the technology in a measured way, understanding its strengths and weaknesses. Rather than a short-term panacea for technology cost and integration challenges, web services are a long-term solution that will gradually speed the development of new applications and integration of the old.

As a result of buyers' realistic expectations, companies are experiencing small and deliberate successes that better the chance of widespread acceptance of web-services technology. These results were reflected in two Sand Hill Group studies. The studies analyzed the current and potential usage of web services and documented 60 case studies of companies that built applications using web services.[6,7] These reports are among the most comprehensive and authoritative pieces of research on the subject.

The top two objectives of companies that participated in these case studies were

- To integrate new externally facing applications with older legacy applications

- To expose and aggregate data from multiple legacy systems in a new web services–based application

Nearly two-thirds of the companies that were profiled implemented web services to decrease either their business or their IT costs and were successful in reaching their goals.

The caveats

This range of benefits may sound overambitious and inflated. Let's make it clear: It is overambitious and inflated. It is too good to be true for most companies. The companies that have succeeded with web services have realistic expectations and projects that are limited in business and technical scope—like any 80-percent solution. Before enthusiasm takes hold, consider that widespread deployment of web services can carry some significant pitfalls. These include:

- **Hype.** Like many new technologies, the vision and the reality of what web services can accomplish have diverged significantly. Certain types of technical problems (such as linking and aggregating data from different web sites) can be solved easily with web services, whereas others (such as creating complex applications using bits of code that are linked over the Web) cannot be implemented easily.

- **Security, integrity, and performance.** Current specifications do little to ensure that applications and data tied together over the Web are secure and will work without fail. Applications have a wide variety of performance characteristics and types; only a few types of applications can be built completely with web services.

- **A lack of contextual (semantic) standards.** Developers use Extensible Markup Language (XML) to describe the piece of data named "the customer." *Semantics* deal with the elements or context that define a customer, including address, credit card number, credit ranking, and other information. Without semantic standards, it is unlikely that web services will reach their potential. Industries such as banking, health care, and retail are creating semantic standards, but these standards are incompatible. In 1998, RosettaNet was formed by electronics manufacturers to create a set of semantic standards. As of 2003, RosettaNet was continuing with its work.

- **Microsoft versus the world.** There are two technology camps in web services: Microsoft .NET and Java 2 Enterprise Edition (J2EE). Like IBM, Microsoft has had a tendency to grab a so-called industry standard and change it "slightly" so it works "better." There is always the possibility that many of the key protocols of the Web could become subverted in this way.

Any one of these difficulties could greatly minimize the benefits and cost reductions realized from web services. In the next 5 to 10 years, I hope these issues will be overcome. Standards wars are forcing both groups to come to a solution. Web-services technology has a better chance of being realized than other standards efforts because it is more aligned with corporate and technological IT pricing and deployment pressures.

INCREASED PRICING PRESSURES

One of the by-products of the Web and the entire movement to a more standard technology stack is the downward pricing pressure that has moved well beyond hardware and hit every market in IT. Buyer behaviors have changed significantly in the last few years— and not just because the post-Internet bubble created a buyers' market. Factors driving down pricing include the following:

- **Low-cost alternatives.** Technology markets are populated with companies that deliver a faster, cheaper price point than competitors. Market and technological factors are accelerating this phenomenon, causing an even swifter drop in overall corporate IT pricing. Buyer savvy and the reluctance to make large purchases of technology also fuel the acceptance of these low-cost alternatives.

- **Microsoft.** Microsoft continues to expand its product line to encompass more corporate IT. Its relentless push to sell products to all levels of IT has made it a competitor of nearly every software company.

- **Freeware.** Linux and open-source code are growing in acceptance among corporations. This software development is putting increased pricing pressures on all software vendors, including Microsoft.

While overall technology spending has climbed during the last 20 years, certain technologies, such as computer hardware, have not grown on a unit-price basis for years (though their performance continues to increase). PC unit prices of less than $1,000 are expected to continue for the foreseeable future. The same pricing stability can be assumed for server computers that run large corporate applications.

The use of inexpensive and widely available microprocessors is permitting companies to build and configure large and powerful computers. Universities and government research centers have led this trend. A new phenomenon called *blade technology*, in which a computing unit becomes processor board that's simple to install and swap out, have started to enter corporate computing centers. Blade computers, built with slide-in PC boards, promise to be cheaper and easier to maintain than conventional servers. VMware, as mentioned in chapter 5, is deploying a mainframe era-type approach to harness and manage these systems.

In late 2003, computer maker Sun Microsystems introduced the concept of *wafer-scale* hardware technology as part of a military-funded R&D effort. Although not expected to be commercialized soon, wafer-scale technology would eliminate the need for printed circuit boards and enable systems to work up to 100 times faster than is possible today. Every few years, innovative companies continue to push the envelope of hardware speeds, driving prices downward.

So far, corporate software has been immune to this trend, but its maturity and continuing consolidation have begun to put it on the same path as its hardware counterparts. The chart on the next page illustrates the historical context of this trend toward price declines.

This type of progression is common to any market: Baseline technology items (e.g., operating systems and browsers) are consolidated first, followed by higher-value ones. For software, these trends are often accelerated because of a combination of technological advances

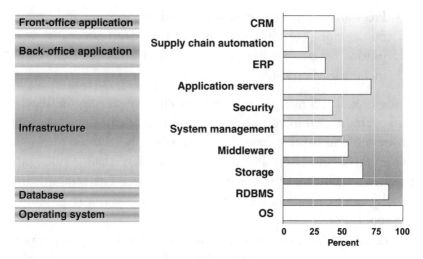

Market share of the top five vendors in different software segments. As technology and products increase in value, so does market fragmentation.[8] At the lowest technology levels, such as operating systems and databases, there is little competition. At the higher-value levels of applications such as CRM, significant market fragmentation still exists. Given that this chart's data is more than two years old, it understates the current degree of consolidation in the different sectors. *Source: McKinsey & Co.*

and easy-to-copy software. Let's look at one of the best examples of how low-cost alternatives can cannibalize a software company.

Generic CADD and other low-cost alternatives

In the 1980s, most major corporations used either expensive mainframe host or engineering workstation equipment for computer-aided design (CAD) to automate manual drafting. Software that could let an engineer draw a simple, 2-D image (as on a piece of paper) could cost as much as $50,000 per seat. The introduction of the PC facilitated the mid-1980s launch of Autodesk, whose initial product was AutoCAD, a PC-based 2-D drafting software package that was sold by distributors for $3,000 or less per seat.

By the late 1980s, the power of the PC—combined with a more sophisticated offering by Autodesk—made AutoCAD the dominant 2-D drafting package. This forced the larger vendors of the time— CADAM, Unigraphics, and Computervision, whose software ran on expensive $20,000 and up Unix-based workstations—to drop their pricing for similar functionality tenfold, offer support for the PC, and support the Autodesk proprietary data format (DXF). PCs became the new platform of choice for simple drafting.

But the price cutting was not over. In the mid-1980s, another company called Generic Software entered the automated design market with a PC-based package called Generic CADD. Generic CADD offered AutoCAD-like functionality for under $100—1/30th the price of the AutoCAD solution. Its business plan and purpose were the same as Autodesk's in its early years: Offer 80 percent of the needed functionality for 20 percent of the price of higher-end offerings. Rather than use distributors, Generic Software sold its product through direct mail and telephone. By 1988, it had sold over 100,000 copies and was beginning to affect the earnings and dominance of Autodesk. In 1989, Generic Software was acquired by Autodesk. It would never again experience the growth or prominence it initially enjoyed.

Although Autodesk killed Generic CADD through benign neglect, the message is obvious: Lower-cost, 80-percent solutions often beat more complete and complex ones. It is a lesson that many vendors continue to ignore—a lesson that is being repeated today in a much broader array of markets for a large range of products. Consider the following:

- **Salesforce.com's Internet-based timesharing.** One of the fastest-growing companies in the enterprise software space is Salesforce.com. Salesforce.com sells sales-force automation and other CRM-related functions through an inexpensive monthly subscription. Rather than force customers to pay huge up-front license fees and then build, implement, and support a complex solution costing millions of dollars, Salesforce.com makes its offerings available at $65 per month per user. By becoming an Internet-based version of mainframe timesharing, Salesforce.com is able to decrease complexity and offer a basic product for a low price. It has more than 100,000 users and over $100 million in revenue. (I will profile Salesforce.com in chapter 11.)

- **Intuit's financial software.** Intuit is one of the dominant companies for personal finance (Quicken) and income tax

(TurboTax) software. It is also one of the largest providers of financial software for small companies (fewer than 50 employees) with its QuickBooks product. It has started to build up this package and outsourced offerings (such as payroll) to support companies with 1,000 employees and specific industries, such as health care, retail, construction, and not-for-profit. Intuit is accomplishing this by providing a software package with the same degree of ease of use and customization as its traditional offering. It is rolling out a variety of inexpensive, simple-to-use and -deploy enterprise software packages.

- **Open-source software.** Open-source software is changing the economics of software buying. It is fundamentally altering the value proposition for end users and in some areas will decrease the market revenue potential for certain sellers of IT products.

Together, all of these trends and products are pushing price points down and changing the fundamentals of buying technology. But there is another factor driving down enterprise pricing— it's called Microsoft.

MICROSOFT: RESISTANCE IS FUTILE

Microsoft can no longer be dismissed by corporations as it was in the early 1990s. Over the last decade, it has made steady incursions into corporate accounts. Microsoft has been able to make this relentless march by leveraging the price/performance advances in hardware as well as its dominant computer desktop position.

Over the last decade, Microsoft has slowly and steadily added capabilities, features, and functions that make an exclusively Microsoft environment an obvious choice for many. Ironically, after decades of trying to escape the proprietary, exclusive clutches of IBM's mainframe technology, companies are comfortably settling into the proprietary, exclusive clutches of Microsoft's PC-based technology.

As Microsoft's corporate IT capabilities have increased, so have its revenues. In 2002, not including desktop sales, nearly 25 percent of Microsoft's revenues were derived from products that fulfill corporate IT needs.

Depending on the type of computing requirement, Microsoft's cost advantage (or disadvantage) over competitors varies. An accepted rule of thumb has been that Microsoft technology is the most appropriate for small workloads and companies, Unix for medium, and IBM mainframe (or what is being called zSeries today) for large.[9] Given Microsoft's strides, this segmentation in 2003 was less clear; it may well disappear by 2007.

At Gartner's Spring Symposium in 2003, a presentation titled "The Future of Windows in the Data Center" concluded that "Managed well, Windows 2000 is nearly as reliable as a Unix system."[10] The areas compared in the next table represent key metrics that are used by IT professionals to rank a technology's suitability. For example, scalability is a measure of the IT load (e.g., how many orders can be taken simultaneously with a single computer system). Microsoft is well on its way to becoming as good as any other provider in this area. Gartner believes that in 2007, more than 6,000 companies will be using Microsoft's high-end operating system (comparable to Unix's or IBM's mainframe operating systems).

Microsoft's capabilities in various IT areas. As this table from Gartner Inc. shows, Microsoft continues to improve the capabilities of its underlying technology, enabling it to handle nearly every IT task. At the same time, its cost model and dependence on Intel technology often permit it to sell products at a much lower price than most of its competitors. *Source: Gartner Inc.*

Microsoft technology feature	2003	2007
Scalability	2,500+ OLTP user references emerge	Non-differentiator
Availability	99.6% or more application, availability references	Non-differentiator
Manageability	Blade management software improves	Competitive market, much improved
Skills availability	Experienced skills gap closing	Non-differentiator
High-end operating system (Datacenter) applications	Less than 200	More than 1,000
Price	Price leader at 16-way processors and below	Price leader up to 32-way processors
Market acceptance	1,000 enterprises using Datacenter in production	6,000+ enterprises using Datacenter in production

Given the often-substantial initial price difference between Microsoft and its competitors, that tells you a lot about where software is going.

Taking on enterprise software

This march toward larger, cheaper, and simpler applications has been relentless and has recently taken Microsoft to the loftiest domain in enterprise software: enterprise applications. Through the $2.4 billion purchase of Great Plains and Navision (renamed Microsoft Business Solutions), Microsoft has established a foothold in the enterprise software space. Beyond traditional ERP packages, Microsoft introduced a CRM package in 2002 that is targeted toward small and medium-sized companies.

While Microsoft insists that it has no plans to take on its larger application partners, such statements ring hollow considering its past. For instance, Microsoft's SQL Server database technology had its genesis in the late 1980s as a low-end derivative of Sybase's relational database system. Today, Sybase is no longer a significant seller of database software, and Microsoft is aggressively competing against the other two dominant database players: IBM and Oracle.

Microsoft has made an art form of adopting the guise of friend turned into competitor. In the mid-1990s, Microsoft made large overtures to SAP. Microsoft Chairman Bill Gates gave a speech at SAP's headquarters in Germany and told its employees that SAP was the most important and best applications partner it had. A few years later, in 1998, I was discussing Microsoft with Hasso Plattner, then CEO and chairman of SAP.

"Hasso, Microsoft is one of your most strategic partners now, right?"

"Yes."

"In five years, will Microsoft still be one of your most strategic partners or one of your biggest competitors?"

Long pause. Plattner was thinking about his response. Then he answered.

"I would prefer not to answer that question."

His refusal to answer the question was the answer. Plattner was no fool.

Microsoft's strategies in applications and other areas of enterprise software follow the same pattern: Start low, work your way up with low initial pricing, and disrupt companies and technologies along the way. Microsoft's detractors may point out that a low-priced product does not necessarily translate into a low-cost solution. A solution encompasses many different costs, including the initial product price, labor, maintenance, custom coding, supplemental software, and hardware. Because of its ability to create pricing "sound bites" that seem attractive on the surface, Microsoft has been able to change the rules of market engagement.

Certain buyers recognize this truth, but it doesn't matter. As discussed in chapter 3, buyers rarely take total cost of ownership (TCO) into account when buying products. For those who do, there are few other obvious choices. When it comes to TCO, which looks at initial and ongoing costs, Microsoft has its fair share of wins and losses. But Microsoft's often-rock-bottom initial cost gets it in the door at major corporations, and this is why Microsoft sees open source, Linux in particular, so threatening. It is another lever that is being used by corporations to cut prices.

IN COMES LINUX

From the bottom to near the top—that was the change in CIO interest in Linux between spring 2002 and spring 2003, according to a Morgan Stanley CIO survey.[11] This result mirrors numerous surveys taken in 2001 and 2002 that revealed nearly 75 percent of all respondents were willing to replace Microsoft-based applications with Linux and other open-source software if available. This figure was up from 50 percent the year before.[12] Whereas the change is sudden and large, it isn't a surprise given the renewed focus on cost-cutting within IT groups. Companies are finding that Linux and the open-source movement can offer significant cost benefits.

Open-source software is moving well beyond a few specific technologies, as the table on the next page shows. It is a movement within the software community to share and develop a wide variety of code that historically has been tightly controlled by its sellers. This software encompasses two important aspects: The first is that it is free (or close to it) to anyone who wants a copy of it and who adheres to some simple agreements. The second is that it can be changed and added to by any company or person with the general idea that these modifications can and will be shared with others. Although this approach goes against the idea of stable code and conflicts with most software business models, it can also permit greater flexibility, better tailored to the individual needs of a company.

Building custom solutions

The ability to get a piece of code free has become an excellent building block for those companies seeking to build custom solutions from an existing and workable base of software. Vendors selling proprietary solutions argue that such actions are foolish. Yet such customization is common and widespread in corporate IT. Many companies (with the notable exception of Microsoft) have started to incorporate aspects of open-source software into their commercial offerings.

A list of open-source software. Open-source software is available for a wide variety of technical and application needs, ranging from browsers and operating systems to ERP and CRM applications. Although the degree of sophistication, functionality, and stability differs greatly, such systems can be used successfully as replacements for certain proprietary products and as building blocks for custom programming efforts.

Technology	Proprietary	Open source
Operating system	Sun (Solaris), Microsoft (Windows), IBM (MVS)	Red Hat, IBM, SUSE, Lindows.com (Linux)
Database	Oracle, IBM (DB2), Microsoft (SQL Server)	MySQL, PostgreSQL, SAP (MaxDB)
Web infrastructure	BEA, CA, IBM, Microsoft	Apache Software Foundation, OpenLDAP Foundation, JBoss
Development tools/languages	Microsoft, IBM, CA, Oracle, Pegasystems, ILOG	IBM (Eclipse), Apache, ActiveState (Perl, others)
Desktop applications	Microsoft (Office, Explorer), IBM (Lotus), Corel (WordPerfect)	Sun (StarOffice), Mozilla (browser), OSA Foundation, OpenOffice (OpenOffice.org)
Content management	EMC (Documentum), Interwoven, Vignette	Zope, Red Hat, OpenCms
Enterprise applications	SAP, Oracle, Microsoft, Siebel	Compiere (ERP and CRM), Ohioedge, Anteil (CRM)

Technology companies are using open source to exploit their existing business models at the expense of competitors. IBM, for example, has been moving its business model from hardware and software to services. In 2003, service revenue represented some 50 percent of all revenue. For IBM customers, application software is but a small portion of the initial technology expenditure. Application software typically represents less than 10 percent of a customer's total lifetime cost for a complex solution.

With open source, IBM is seeking to capture a larger portion of what a company spends on services to deploy and maintain a complex software solution. Others—such as Sun Microsystems, with its StarOffice desktop—support open source as a mechanism to attack and weaken key Microsoft revenue streams. SAP uses open source to promote and increase the value of its own application solutions at the expense of core revenue streams of competitors.

In spring 2003, SAP announced a partnership with Swedish technology company MySQL AB whereby it would turn over development of its open-source database (Adabas D, which it acquired from Software AG in 1999, now named MaxDB) to MySQL. It also announced that its application suite would support MySQL's database technology, giving its customers a lower-cost database compared with IBM, Microsoft, and Oracle.

As open source has become more acceptable to buyers, it too is being used to effectively compete with and point out pricing weaknesses of competitors.

Open source on a large scale

Initially, open source was used deep within IT departments. These groups have the technical prowess to manage and evaluate such technologies, understanding where they are to be widely deployed and where they should have limited use. Google is at one end of the open-source use scale. To process more than 200 million Internet searches a day, Google claims to possess the world's largest Linux server cluster, with over 10,000 servers. It stores more than 3 billion web pages on its index and is currently the dominant Internet search provider. Because it executes only a single type of business function,

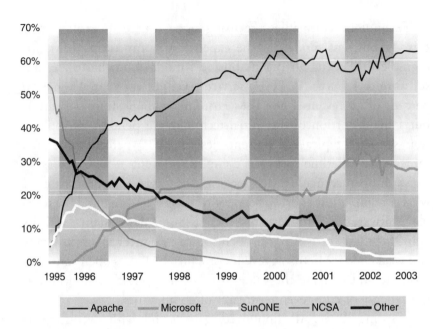

Market share of web servers between August 1995 and May 2003. ASF's Apache web server has been the leading web server software on the market for the past seven years. Over 60 percent of all web sites use this web server to store and host Internet (or HTTP) pages. *Source: Netcraft (http://www.netcraft.com).*

it stripped all unneeded code out of Linux to maximize the performance and speed of its technology.[13]

The use of open source is not limited to a few companies that want to be on the edge. Companies that are using Linux for commercial applications include Winnebago Industries, Merrill Lynch & Co, and L. L. Bean. In fact, the Apache web server, currently a core component of the Apache Software Foundation (ASF),[14] has widespread use around the globe, as the graph above illustrates.

The growing use of technologies such as Apache and the continued expansion of other open-source technologies are changing the way traditional vendors provide value. Open-source solutions have started to emerge on the desktop as well.

Open source on the desktop

In spring 2003, the city of Munich decided to replace its IT infrastructure and desktops with Linux-based solutions. In 2004, the city plans to start replacing over 14,000 Windows-based PCs and desktop software with Linux-based solutions. While it is unclear whether these solutions will save the city money in the long run, the decision has forced Microsoft to consider how it can compete. A memo leaked to *The New York Times* indicates that Microsoft set up a $180 million fund in its 2003 fiscal year to combat Linux and other less expensive alternatives.[15]

Sun Microsystems is also doing its best to combat Microsoft's monopoly on desktop software. In 1999, it purchased the Star-Office product, which consists of word processing, spreadsheet, presentation, and personal productivity software. StarOffice runs on Windows, Linux, and Solaris computers. In large corporate volumes, Sun will license a copy for as little as $25. By the end of 2002, Sun boasted 70,000 registered users and 8.5 million downloads of the software.

Open-source technology has even made it to the consumer sector. Wal-Mart's web site (http://www.walmart.com) is selling PCs for as little as $200 that are configured with a variety of open-source offerings (operating system, browser, and personal productivity software). Today, this type of computer is meant only for the technologically savvy. The same observation, however, was made of most computers before browser-based user interfaces became common in the late 1990s. It is a fair assumption that within a decade, open systems–based PCs will be as easy to use and set up as Windows desktops.

Open source ultimately forces a vendor to switch its investment and revenue strategy from the front end to the back end. With hardware vendors looking to sell more support services, open source looks like a potential cash cow. What a vendor may lose in hardware or software license fees (either to open-source or low-cost software alternatives), it hopes to pick up in long-term support contracts and consulting. These factors are permitting buyers to play vendors against one another, forcing margins and long-term pricing downward.

IT PAYS TO BE SIMPLE

Software standards, low-cost offerings, and a more accepted view of the 80-percent solution are changing the dynamics of software spending models. Companies are discovering that a combination of new web-based solutions and low-cost technologies allows them to cut their IT costs significantly.

This move toward simplicity was illustrated in fall 2003 by the announcement that Siebel and IBM would jointly sell inexpensive, easy-to-use, hosted CRM services for less than $100 per month per user, much like the model adopted by Salesforce.com. Formerly, the two collaborated only on delivering highly complex, expensive, customized systems. Like other sellers of technology, they have started to realize the power of simplicity.

The economic benefits of simplicity, as illustrated by IBM and Siebel, can be seen in the chart below. The IT cost for a given business function (e.g., entering orders, dispatching service personnel, calculating risk) using complex technologies is often high. The complexity of the solution helps to drive up costs. Therefore, companies are taking new approaches to reduce IT complexity. As a result, the same business function is delivered at a lower cost.

Because managing the constant fire drills of keeping systems up and running is time consuming, simplicity helps IT groups

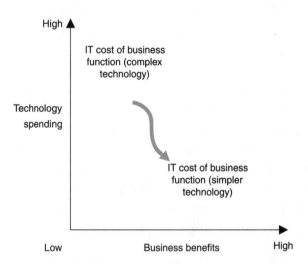

Simplicity pays. The lack of IT complexity does deliver a small degree of business benefit to IT organizations. Companies that execute a simpler and less costly technology base will obtain increased IT productivity from executing the same business function at a lower cost.

transform themselves into more efficient business organizations. Fighting fires leaves little time for strategic imperatives.

For buyers, standardized strategies should be an essential part of any IT toolkit. This is not to imply that failures and problems will not occur. More than a few companies have had to write off large, Internet-based investments as well as development plans, and more than a few Microsoft-based solutions have failed. These technologies must be used properly in order to be effective.

Some companies will not embrace these changes. "This is yet another round of the technology shell game promulgating another malformed savior as a quick fix against a prophesied doomsday," some IT managers will say. And who knows? Such views may be correct. History reveals many examples of broken promises and failed predictions; nevertheless, a growing number of companies are willing to take chances.

Despite the fact that open-source or low-cost software can backfire, it is changing market dynamics considerably. It is putting the price models of many IT suppliers at risk. Some sellers believe they have found the answer (and potential revenue replacement) in service offerings. But there is a catch. A new dynamic in delivering IT service has arrived—and it's from out of town. Way out of town, as you'll see in the next chapter.

SURVIVAL GUIDE
FOR BUYERS

SIMPLER, CHEAPER IT SOLUTIONS

While companies cannot simply swap out expensive for inexpensive technology, they can take certain steps to begin the journey toward simpler, cheaper IT solutions:

- **Look closely at how the Internet can simplify integration/programming.** While the Internet is no panacea, it offers ample opportunities to use its technology to ease integration of data and processes. Service-based programming techniques will decrease the cost of change and maintenance over time. Building or integrating applications using a variety of web-service protocols and standards should help companies increase productivity in the short term and decrease maintenance costs in the long term.

- **Use standard technology and methods.** Seek to reduce rather than increase the complexity of IT systems through the use of standard technology and methods. Minimizing the number of providers and approaches to business problems can save large sums of money and make IT more effective. Attempt to utilize more standardized interfaces and procedures in the management of IT solutions. Build an IT infrastructure that has in-house and external providers that can be swapped out or easily interfaced at will.

- **Look for opportunities to swap down.** Take an inventory of systems that could be replaced with lower-cost items. Be careful, though; consider all costs, including training and end-user acceptance, before making the jump. You may have many opportunities, particularly when you need large upgrades or process changes, to swap out higher-cost solutions/services for lower-cost ones. Identify high-cost, low-value assets within the IT portfolio, and look for eventual replacements.

- **Explore open-source alternatives.** Open-source software can provide an excellent starting point for custom development. For narrowly defined needs, open-systems software can offer compelling values. Most software segments have some type of open-source offering, so look around and compare freeware to more traditional choices. Fully understand support requirements before jumping in.

- **Negotiate prices using different benchmarks, open-source systems, and other low-price solutions.** The solutions with the lowest initial cost may not be the least expensive long term, but they can provide an excellent pricing lever during negotiating processes for new technologies and services. Don't be fooled by sales-force propaganda insisting that prices will never be as good as they are now. All trends point to declining prices in software and services. Use alternative, lower-cost benchmarks for all processes.

- **Consider simple, 80-percent solutions.** In many cases, it is better to implement an 80-percent solution that addresses the core business processes without many of the complex bells and whistles that drive up costs and complexity. Get an agreement from users and technologists to list the "nice-to-have" versus the "got-to-have" features and functions of solutions. This is more difficult than you might imagine—a diligent leader will be needed to facilitate this process.

SURVIVAL GUIDE
FOR SELLERS

SIMPLER, CHEAPER IT SOLUTIONS

Sellers have a different list of concerns; new buying behaviors will force them to alter their offerings and price points. Sellers must:

- **Understand the economics of markets and products.** The spell-checker market disappeared in the mid-1980s when that function became embedded in word processing software. Over time, so will many other features and functions. These commodities will either be embedded into a larger suite or available in an open-source version. Unless your business model is set up to exploit commodity-based pricing, have a realistic view of what will represent value to buyers in the future. Cost models will need to be shifted downward for many companies, with a drastic reassignment of resources and people.

- **Be ready to cannibalize your product offerings.** Companies must understand how to reinvent their products and business models in light of the continuing standardization of products and services. Over the next decade, much of the enterprise software business will fall into this category. It is better to cannibalize your own product lines before your competitors do. The other alternative is to buy out a lower-priced competitor and let it wither away. This does not ensure long-term survival, but it may give you some short-term breathing room to revamp your business model.

- **Never ignore an inferior company or technology.** A good number of technology companies fall from grace because they ignore an inferior approach that becomes more mature over time. Such ignorance has cost companies such as IBM to lose market share and revenue. Never underestimate the power of a low-cost, easy-to-use technology. Look to incorporate such capabilities into your own solutions to increase customer loyalty.

SURVIVAL GUIDE
FOR SELLERS

- Remember that unless you have a well-defined niche, Microsoft will become the enemy. As Microsoft marches up the enterprise software stack, it will embed and offer more features and functions within its solution at a lower initial cost (at least when it attempts to crack a market). Within a decade, few software sectors will exist that won't compete directly with Microsoft. Companies must choose between two strategies: establish a strong niche that is either too small or too hard for Microsoft to penetrate effectively, or execute a broad strategy extremely well.

CHAPTER SEVEN

OFFSHORING:
THE NEW TREND

There are a number of well-meaning Luddites in the U.S. who still believe that India is only capable of providing low-cost programmers, who know nothing about business and don't even speak English; to such people, it may come as a shock to learn that [over] half of the SEI-CMM Level 4 and Level 5 [highest-quality certification] IT organizations in the world are located in India.
—Edward Yourdon, noted author
and software engineering authority[1]

Looking at this in the extreme case, we will be spending hundreds of millions of dollars in offshoring.
—CTO, Fortune 50 company

I T WAS A SMALL ITEM buried in the back of the business section of the local newspaper. Sykes Enterprise Inc., a Tampa, FL-based company that specializes in providing outsourcing and consulting services (with a focus on technology companies), had added 2,300 call center seats or terminals (computer and telephone stations for workers) in low-cost labor markets during the year 2002. This addition brought its total number of non-U.S. call center seats to 3,300. (Each seat is used by more than one employee.) At the beginning of 2003, Sykes had nearly 16,000 employees and was planning to add 3,400 more seats in the Philippines, Costa Rica, and India in 2003.

"Sykes believes its future is in what it calls offshore markets or at least those where an overwhelming majority of workers are college graduates, staff turnover is relatively low, and wages are a fraction of those earned by American employees," the article went on to say. By the middle of 2004, Sykes plans to have more call center seats and capacity in "low-paid, well-educated" countries than in the United States.[2]

Sykes is embracing a new trend called *offshoring*—and it is not alone. Offshoring, either directly or through a third party, involves the use of labor in countries where workers may be paid a tenth or less of what they are paid in the United States. The potential for savings is huge, considering the difference between the cost of U.S. versus Indian or other labor for jobs in programming, application maintenance, and technical support. Offshoring allows companies to cut personnel and service costs (both internal and sourced to third parties) by 40 percent or more.

OFFSHORING IS HERE TO STAY

Offshoring is not a new idea. In 1992, it was eloquently expressed by Edward Yourdon, a leading software engineer, in his book *Decline and Fall of the American Programmer*. Yourdon recognized that the seeds of low-cost, high-quality foreign labor were being sown at U.S. universities such as MIT and Stanford and that India's university system was maturing to top-rate status. Although he recanted some of his findings in a 1996 book, *Rise and Resurrection of the American Programmer*, he had accurately identified an early trend—one that is now beginning to have a large impact on U.S. IT employment and salaries. Today, Yourdon is on the board of directors of iGATE, a $300 million publicly traded Indian firm specializing in offshore development, business-process outsourcing, and IT software management and deployment.

The potential for change is huge. According to U.S. Department of Commerce figures, in 2001, U.S. companies capitalized $120 billion on contracted and internal IT labor. More than double this amount is spent on technical support and other labor expenses. Combined, companies in the United States spent more than $400 billion on labor associated with IT in 2001.

As you can see in the table below, according to the Information Technology Association of America (ITAA), in 2003 there were just over 10 million IT workers in the United States—nearly 8 percent of the total U.S. labor force. Average salaries ranged from $84,000 per year for managers, to $63,000 for a staff member, to $44,000 for a customer help desk specialist.[3] While jobs were plentiful in the late 1990s, over the past few years IT job growth and wage gains have flattened.

The ITAA data indicates that the overall market is still growing but at a slow pace. Although software services grew, the American Electronics Association (AEA) found that over 560,000 high-tech jobs were lost during 2001 and 2002.[4] According to the U.S. Bureau of Labor, more than 200,000 jobs have been lost in computer and mathematical occupations. An increasing number of these

Net total IT job counts in 2003 by category. With more than 10 million employees, IT-related professions are a major contributor to high-value jobs in the U.S. economy. Over 85 percent of these jobs are with buyers rather than providers of IT. Source: ITAA.

IT job category	Number of employees
Programming/software engineering	2,144,377
Technical support	1,904,842
Other	1,290,719
Enterprise systems	1,113,883
DBMS development/administration	1,011,331
Web development/administration	885,070
Network design/administration	729,417
Digital Media	694,251
Technical writing	538,759
Total	10,312,649

job losses are due to business and technological factors that cannot be changed. Various economic downturns during the 1980s led manufacturing companies to outsource jobs and processes abroad. IT spending and jobs are similarly poised to migrate overseas during the next 20 years.[5]

But unlike manufacturing workers, technologists have been sowing the seeds of their unemployment. The nature of IT work combined with broadly available communications (both voice and network) and inexpensive PCs have permitted IT professionals in the United States to lead the way toward establishing virtual and remote workplaces. The irony is that the fruits of their ingenuity are now being enjoyed by India and other such countries, whose IT employees are replacing U.S. employees by the score, at a fraction of the price. Once you are remote, it doesn't matter whether you are in India or Indiana.

"With the proper degree of [software-enabled] collaboration, you should be able to give up to 70 percent of all work to offshore personnel," according to Vincent Massol, technical director for Pivolis, a Paris-based company that sells a toolset and services for managing offshore development and collaboration. "It's a much larger number than most people believe." Massol believes that his clients are considering moving upward of 50 percent of IT work to offshore providers.

Large labor savings

Fueling this change is a rapidly growing IT infrastructure and skill set being led by India and followed closely by China, Russia, and other nations.[6] As a group, these nations are promoting a low-cost, high-quality labor pool that can be used to supplement, or supplant, internal and external service providers in the United States and Western Europe.

"We believe that we can offer companies a 20 to 50 percent [labor] savings," said Chandrasekaran Natarajan, corporate vice president of Tata Consultancy Services in Mumbai, India. In 2003, Tata was the largest professional services firm in Asia, with more than 20,000 employees and revenue of $811 million. In the programming area alone, Tata says that it can save a company at least 40 to 50

Global IT labor pool costs. Offshored labor will have a huge impact on wages paid to employees and contractors over the next few years. High-end U.S.-based consultants will be forced to slash certain rates by one third or more, while U.S. employees will find raises limited. The numbers here are average cost per hour. They are negotiated on many different bases and vary significantly based on volume, region, and skill set. *Source: JetStream Group and Wapiti LLC.*

Labor pool	Per-hour personnel cost (in $U.S.)	
	2002	2006
High-end U.S. (IBM, Accenture, etc.)	$175	$110
Regional U.S. (Keane, Crowe Chizek, etc.)	$125	$90
Independent contractor	$80	$50
Internal IT staff (burdened cost)	$45	$45
On-site, Indian offshore (TCS, Infosys, etc.)	$50	$60
Off-site, Indian offshore	$15	$20
Emerging offshore (BridgeQuest [Russia], ASTI Shanghai [China], SPI Technologies [Philippines])	$10	$15

percent. Such a statement may seem outrageous, but the difference in salaries and associated costs makes such claims easy to believe.

As the table above shows, there are differing tiers of service and cost. Service providers such as IBM and Accenture take on large, costly projects that require a great deal of custom (and typically high-priced) technical and business-process assistance. They do little tactical programming and stick to high-value efforts. The next tier, which includes such firms as Keane and Crowe Chizek, are oriented toward servicing the smaller company or a larger one with a well-defined or bounded job, such as installing software to automate a warehouse.

Some Indian offshore providers are planning to emulate the high-end models of IBM and Accenture (for business-process reengineering or outsourcing) in terms of the services they offer. At the low end of the cost spectrum, offshore companies are emerging that specialize in writing detailed, highly specified software code and thus act as low-cost body shops.

The impact of these software providers will be an equalization in pricing over the next three years or so as offshore companies find their cost models increasing due to the addition of foreign employees from the United States and Western Europe to their payrolls. In the meantime, large U.S. consulting companies and systems integrators are being forced to set up operations in India, China, and Russia to create a pool of low-cost labor.

These changes are having a powerful impact on cost structures. In 2002, U.S. consulting companies had a pricing structure that was between 3 and 12 times that of their Indian counterparts. To compete, U.S.-based companies will need to change what and how they charge. JetStream CEO Vinnie Mirchandani predicts that in the next few years the blended hourly consulting rate for traditional consultants will need to hit $80 per hour to stay competitive. To reach this rate, U.S. consulting companies will supplement their staffs with offshore labor pools to decrease client billing rates.

A new address for IT workers

In 2001, many companies were not aware of offshoring. But by the end of 2003, nearly every U.S. technology provider had examined it in one way or another; buyers, too, were quickly considering the potential of offshoring.

"Generally speaking, the quality of deliverables I see out of India is higher than what I would see from U.S. folks," said David Wood of Otis Elevator, a division of United Technologies Corp. "This is largely due to the India IT industry's focus on quality over the last 10 or more years."[7] Wood has more than a decade of offshoring experience under his belt and set up a development center in India during the early 1990s.

By 2005, General Electric (GE) expects to save more than $1 billion via offshoring software development, call center support, and key technical R&D. In 2003, it had over 19,000 employees in India—11,000 had jobs in back-office functions, and 7,600 worked in software development.[8] In fall 2003, GE opened a $64 million R&D center in China, with over 500 employees.

Other major companies, including Citibank, Procter & Gamble, American Express, Dell, and Prudential, have outsourced IT and business processes offshore. These companies recognize offshoring as a key strategy to reduce their IT costs.

"There were a couple of catalysts that caused us to investigate offshoring [in 2001]," said Scott, a CTO for a Fortune 50 company. "The first was a partnership with a company that did a lot of offshoring. They were having success with it. Cost cutting was always a focus, and then there was the issue of quality.

"We recognized that we didn't have much beyond CMM1 [a quality standard] in our organization," he continued. "Offshoring was a means by which we could significantly increase our software quality." Once Scott's company decided to use offshore resources for IT, it put together an evaluation process and ultimately decided to use a few key providers in India. Scott felt that, beyond software quality and cost, it was important that the partners not harm his company's brand.

"When we were evaluating the cost models and companies [in India], we had to ensure that the companies we were dealing with shared the same type of values for employees that we did," said Scott. "In many cases we found them to be extremely progressive. They had [HR] practices and benefits that only now are beginning to be adopted by Western companies."

Scott expects that his company will offshore more than $100 million of IT services to India in 2004: "Ultimately, we may do as much as $200 million to $300 million a year. We believe we can take away a lot of cost in all areas of programming." In programming, Scott is saving between 40 and 50 percent and getting higher-quality service than he is able to acquire from internal groups within the company.

And he believes that is only the beginning: "The next step is to use [offshore companies] for business-process redesign. It's good to get a new and different perspective on things."

Call centers and customer support for IT and other business areas is another offshoring opportunity that is becoming well accepted by buyers of technology. Hourly call center labor rates of $30 in the United States are $4.50 in the Philippines and $4 in India. For example, one financial services client was handling 1.6 million technical and customer support calls a year at a cost of $6.4 million, or $4 per call. It was looking for ways to decrease its call center costs. It was determined that, by using a combination of voice-recognition technology and India- or Philippine-based call centers, annual costs would be decreased to $2.3 million, with a savings of more than 60 percent. Needless to say, the client decided to pursue the offshore option. In 2003, a total of 100 full-time U.S. jobs were cut from that company.

Advantages for software producers

Software companies are also seeing the advantages of offshoring and are aggressively moving resources out of the United States. In a typical software company, more than half of the employees deliver programming or related services to customers. Offshoring offers these companies the opportunity to cut labor expenses significantly. Here are some examples:

- PeopleSoft opened a lab and development center in Bangalore, India, and anticipates having some 300 employees by the end of 2004. It expects to decrease its associated personnel costs by 35 percent and increase customer responsiveness by 25 percent.[9]

- SAP plans to double its Indian workforce in the next 3 years (to 2,000 software professionals) and is moving part of its business-process outsourcing operation to Bangalore.

- Intel expects to have more than 3,000 engineers working in Bangalore by 2005.

- By fall 2003, Oracle had more than 3,500 employees in India and had announced plans to rapidly increase this number.[10]

Many software companies have announced similar plans.

Governments pitch in

Some foreign governments are taking a proactive role in creating attractive centers of technology for U.S. companies. For example, the Indian government has set up special software technology parks in such places as Noida, Navi Mumbai, Pune, Gandhinagar, and Bangalore, with facilities and communication capabilities rivaling those in Silicon Valley.

These technology parks and the demand for high-quality, low-cost services have allowed Indian providers to grow rapidly. The five largest IT software and services firms in India (Tata, Infosys Technologies, Wipro Technologies, Satyam Computer Services, and HCL Technologies) had a combined revenue of $2.4 billion in

2002. They are key players in the 20 percent-plus annual growth rate of this sector.

China has also created similar zones, though its exports of software and services pale compared to those of India. Although China is behind India in software offshoring, no one is writing off its potential impact in the decades to come.

Offshoring: how much, how fast?

Analyst groups are also predicting a boom in offshoring. Forrester Research expects that in the next 15 years more than 3.3 million service jobs and over $130 billion in annual wages will move from the United States to other countries.[11] A joint report from the National Association of Software and Service Companies (NASSCOM) and McKinsey predicts that by 2008, Indian-based IT outsourcing services (both technical programming and customer support) will reach between $21 billion and $24 billion, employing 1.1 million Indians.[12] Other research firms have similar, and sometimes even more aggressive, views on the topic.

This rapid corporate change in behavior is startling, but the events witnessed by prime offshoring exporters are more remarkable. Although U.S. spending and employment in IT was flattening between 2000 and 2003, offshoring business was steadily growing, most notably in India, followed by China, Russia, and other countries. NASSCOM expects that India will have more than $12 billion in software and IT-service exports in 2003—over $9 billion of that to the United States, as shown on the chart on the next page.

The cost differentials between U.S. and Indian companies imply that the IT exports of India to the United States in 2002 displaced between $20 billion and $30 billion of U.S. spending and salaries. When we project that out to 2008, U.S. companies could potentially displace over $70 billion in IT costs to India just in offshoring. According to NASSCOM, by 2006 India will have 850,000 software developers, up from 270,000 in 2000. The Chinese Software Industry Association claims that it will have nearly 1.6 million software developers by 2006 (up from 280,000 in 2000).[14]

Even if all of this growth is not realized, the magnitude of a new and motivated global IT workforce will put increased wage and

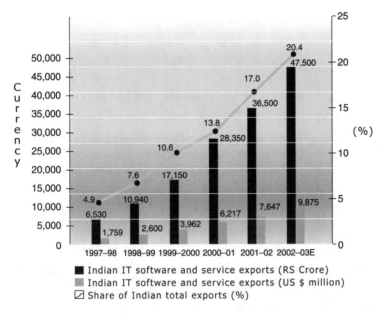

Indian IT software and service exports: 1997–2003. Between 1997 and 2003, IT software and service exports increased from less than $2 billion to nearly $10 billion, or 20 percent of India's total world exports. Much of this growth has come from exports to the United States and is increasing at annual rates in excess of 20 percent.[13]
Source: NASSCOM.

quality pressure on U.S. workers. The focus on university training abroad is a case in point.

The push for higher education

The push for higher education (with a focus on technology) continues to accelerate in India, China, Russia, and other countries. For example, India, with more than 1 billion people, is graduating over 1.5 million people per year from its universities; of these graduates, 170,000 have engineering degrees and speak English, and an additional 60,000 or more have degrees in computer science and applied math. In contrast, the United States, with more than 280 million people, is graduating 1.75 million people per year from its universities, and slightly over 170,000 graduate with engineering and computer science degrees.[15]

And even these figures are misleading. Nearly half of all graduate degrees in computer science and engineering in the United States are granted to foreign nationals, many of whom come from India and China.

China becomes a player

China is another nation that has great potential to export low-cost technology services to the United States and Western Europe, though it has significant challenges to overcome first. Its fast growth in GDP and GNI (gross net income) is creating a market of consumers and wealth where none existed five years ago; see the table below. The rapid increase in Internet users and establishment of fixed and mobile telephone lines are key indicators of a culture that has moved from isolation to broad collaborative communications.

What is intriguing about China is the speed by which it has been able to add infrastructure and high-tech capabilities. For example, more than 600 multinationals have set up shop in China's Suzhou New District (SNU), which was created in 1990.[16]

Together, these factors reflect a readiness and a maturing technical infrastructure that will permit China to take full advantage of its potential to sell IT services abroad within the next decade. IT is a cornerstone of China's Tenth Five-Year Development Plan (2001–2005); the government has declared the information industry to be a "pillar industry."

But the realization of this potential will not come without a struggle. China is well respected and known for its manufacturing

Key economic statistics for China.[17] Although a common view of China is that it has too many insurmountable problems to become an economic threat to the United States, key statistics show that it has made huge strides in the last few years in key technology and communications areas. *Source: World Bank.*

Key economic statistics for China	1997	2000	2001
GDP growth (annual percentage)	8.8%	8%	7.3%
GNI per capita	$710	$840	$890
High-technology exports (% of manufactured exports)	12.7%	18.4%	20.4%
Internet users	400,000	22.5 million	33.7 million
Personal computers (per 1,000 people)	6	15.9	19
Fixed and mobile phone lines (per 1,000 people)	67	178	248

prowess, yet India excels in the area of IT knowledge. Chinese universities have only about 37,000 computer science and applied math graduates per year (compared with 60,000 in India), far short of the supply needed to meet internal and external demands.

Even though China is currently behind India in IT skills and knowledge, it is expected to be a major force in offshoring in the coming years.[18] In 2003, the governments of India and China announced a number of programs designed to facilitate economic exchange, with a focus on IT.[19,20] These programs—as well as the perception widely held by American companies that Chinese and Indian quality is inferior where technology is concerned—fuel the allegations by some that the offshoring phenomenon is overstated. Such allegations are clearly inaccurate, as we discuss in the next section.

QUALITY RULES

As the old saying goes, you get what you pay for. Many companies, however, are finding that the overall experience and quality of Indian-based software and service providers is better compared to that provided by their domestic counterparts. As is reflected in the table below, India has a large group of powerful software companies that have a high CMM rating, a quality metric that is being used increasingly by the software industry.[21] More than 65 percent of all CMM Level 4 and 5 certifications (which represent the highest levels of quality) in the world are held by Indian-based organizations.[22] (A few of these companies have corporate headquarters in the United States.) Large military and government contractors such as Boeing,

CMM worldwide rankings for Levels 4 and 5. India has a staggering lead in Software Engineering Institute (SEI) CMM Level 4 and 5 quality certification compared to the rest of the world. Nearly two-thirds of certified sites reside in India (as of August 2003). In the United States, fewer than 10 of the sites are for commercial software development. A few U.S. commercial software developers, however, have CMM Level 4/5–compliant sites located in India and other countries.

CMM worldwide rankings	CMM Level 4	CMM Level 5	Total
India	61 sites	81 sites	142 sites
U.S.	21 sites	31 sites	52 sites
Rest of world	11 sites	9 sites	20 sites

Computer Sciences Corp. (CSC), Lockheed Martin, and IBM's Federal Systems Division account for the vast majority of CMM Level 4 and 5 certified sites in the United States.

Mike Laven, the COO of KW International, a London-based company selling risk-management software to energy companies, said the quality of his Indian offshore partners' output, beyond just the cost, led him to take on an offshore partner. "We have to move from fixed to variable cost [based on the industry they sell to and variance in growth]. By moving to an offshore provider, we have seen a reduction in our technology cost of 50 percent." Quality was a concern to Laven, but "our Indian provider was so superior in quality… that the question of choosing them was easy."

"The mindset [of prospective customers concerning quality] is the largest problem we have…. After 9/11, many of our major customers were surprised to find that we had many more resources and plans for disaster recovery than they had," according to Tata's Natarajan. Tata has the largest number of CMM Level 4/5 sites in the world.

Given this data, it would seem that the allegations that offshore work is of poor quality are unfounded.

WHAT ARE THE PITFALLS?

Offshoring may sound too good to be true for an IT manager trying to cut costs. It does create risks that are not readily understood, including the potential for sabotage and political/economic unrest in key countries like China, India, and Russia. Becoming overly dependent on offshoring without a good backup plan is more foolish than not looking to reduce IT costs via offshoring at all. Companies need to adopt a balanced view so that the correct mix of skills is offshored.

Companies must also be diligent in managing the offshoring process. Over a decade ago, outsourcing was heralded as the best way to cut IT costs and permitted companies to focus on their core competencies. After giving outsourcing a try, many companies have discovered that it can lead to increased costs and decreased levels of service. These failed expectations are due to two factors: poor management of outsourcing contracts and the inability of companies to determine the proper mix of contractors and in-house staff.

The companies that have found success with outsourcing are able to identify these problems early on and manage them accordingly. Industries ranging from financial services to automobile manufacturers are able to do this well with their suppliers, but few IT groups have mastered the process.

The ability to collaborate well with different groups will be key for IT groups. For example, one of Pivolis's clients, a financial vendor, worked on a project that had 10 developers on site in London and 60 working from India. "The key to success is methodology and tools so you can do software collaboration offshore," according to Massol. "You create two teams, and they work together on a daily basis with all the best practices, frameworks, and methodology kept at the customer site." He added that the customer was able to reduce its cost of programming by more than 50 percent using this approach.

Stories from companies that have successfully cracked the offshoring nut all resonate with the fact that it is a long and difficult process that requires diligent change and quality management, good teamwork, and a strategic mindset. Companies should examine offshoring with a focus on the risks as well as the rewards, no differently than they would any other type of business problem.

JOB GROWTH?

The changes outlined in this chapter promise to have a significant impact on the U.S. economy and job growth. The U.S. Bureau of Labor predicts that, compared to other sectors, computer and data-processing service companies will experience the fastest wage and salary employment growth between 2000 and 2010.[23] Employment for these sellers of services is projected to increase at an annual rate of 6.4 percent, from 2.1 million workers in 2000 to 3.9 million workers in 2010.

Many companies, however, are not increasing their IT staffs. Paula, a client in the services industry, said it this way: "Right now we have taken 20 percent of our people [software programmers and support staff] and moved offshore. In the next two years it will go to at least 50 percent."

Statements like these make it hard to believe that labor statistics are telling the whole story, particularly when the top occupations for growth are examined.[24] Of the top 10 occupations listed, only 4 pay relatively well: customer service representatives, registered nurses, computer support specialists, and computer software engineers. Of these four, only nursing is not being aggressively offshored.

As you can see in the chart below, manufacturing employment changed significantly due to the combination of a recession and accelerated offshoring, but only in the last few years. The potential changes in IT employment could be more dramatic and faster than those in manufacturing. Moving manufacturing capabilities requires a large shift in capital resources as well as transportation. In addition, labor costs (as a percentage of the total cost of a manufactured product) vary greatly.

Such is not the case with IT. Given the growth of high-speed networks, the Internet, and high-quality, low-cost offshore companies, the movement of IT-related labor to non-U.S. countries is limited only by the number of people willing to work. IT and other service-related employment could shift from the United States at a much faster rate than seen in the manufacturing sector. And, a higher percentage of total IT costs is associated with labor than with the raw materials that go into an IT solution.

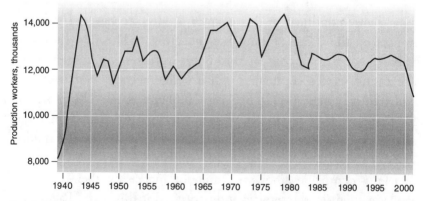

Total number of production workers in the United States since 1939. Production worker employment in manufacturing companies fluctuated between 12 million and 14 million for 30 years after World War II, before settling at about 12.5 million for 20 years. A fast drop of 1.5 million workers occurred between 1999 and today. *Source: Bureau of Labor Statistics.*

Over the next decade, the key focus of offshoring will be not the wholesale movement of IT jobs but rather the emergence of India, China, the Philippines, Russia, and other countries as low-cost, high-quality alternative labor pools that put pressure on U.S. wage and job growth in IT. Domestic help desk agents and Java programmers may well become the machine tool operators and blacksmiths of the 21st century. At the very least, they will not enjoy the high salaries and job security that they experienced during the 1990s.

That is not to say that IT professionals will have no job opportunities in the United States, but I believe that they will work for less money doing different jobs, some of which they were not trained for initially. Technology transfer cannot be stopped—short of introducing punitive legislation. Countries that have relied on such measures, such as Japan, typically solve a short-term issue at the expense of creating a long-term problem.

Labor and IT productivity

As companies look to relocate more of their jobs to foreign shores, IT productivity is expected to increase dramatically. This doesn't mean that companies should offshore everything; that approach

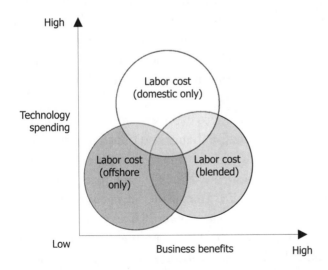

Business benefits per technology dollar spent as a function of labor costs. Companies that look to blend domestic and offshore labor will increase their IT productivity. Moving to an offshore-only labor pool is potentially dangerous and could result in higher costs in other areas.

would echo the mistake companies made a decade ago with out-sourcing. Rather, companies should deploy IT resources in a mixed fashion and consider offshoring between 40 and 70 percent of IT services (either directly or via a third party).

As the chart on the previous page shows, companies that choose to have a domestic-only labor force will experience higher costs than companies that adopt a blended approach. If a company moves all its IT services to an offshore model, the IT cost might be lower, but the company will have to deal with a lack of strong customer and corporate contact as well as the problems of managing such an extreme way of deploying IT resources. In certain situations, the cost of offshored resources could even be higher than that of domestic. Blending these resources will give companies the best of both worlds in quality, responsiveness, core competencies and cost.

IGNORANCE IS BLISS

The common attitude toward the IT capabilities of India reminds me of how U.S. automobile manufacturers (and consumers) viewed Japanese automakers in the 1970s and '80s. A story about die changes sticks indelibly in my mind. Dies are massive pieces of steel that are propelled with great force to stamp out parts like fenders and bumpers. One of the reasons U.S. automakers had long production runs of certain models was that a die change (to accommodate a different car model or style) typically took an entire 8-hour work shift (or longer).

In the early 1980s, American auto executives heard a rumor that Japanese autoworkers were able to change a die in five minutes or less. Even though they did not believe this was possible, they sent a team of engineers over to investigate. When the engineers returned, they confirmed that the rumor was true. Other teams were sent, and they all came back with the same answer: Japanese autoworkers *could* change a die in five minutes or less—in some cases, in less than one minute. It took the U.S. auto industry well over a decade to catch on—and catch up.

Certain IT groups—both buyers and sellers—are in denial about how the industry is changing. They believe that once the economic malaise of 2002–2003 is over, good times will roll. Good times *will* roll, but the question is how and for whom.

The migration of jobs to other shores may be the straw that breaks the back of IT's big spending spree. When the domestic effect of increased offshoring is combined with a pared-back view of IT spending, as well as low-cost hardware and software, the prospects for the future are a technological paradise lost.

The gold rush of unbridled spending growth for IT has been tapped out.

SURVIVAL GUIDE
FOR BUYERS

OFFSHORING

When looking at offshoring, companies should take the following steps:

- **Create and communicate a strategy for offshoring.** Offshoring is not just throwing money and resources abroad. Keep in mind that your initial efforts to create an offshoring strategy will require a great deal of time and skill. Synergy between you and the offshore provider is essential.

- **Identify key areas for offshoring.** For offshoring to be successful, you must determine what stays and what goes. For most organizations, small tactical projects are the best place to start. As your successes mount, you can expand your offshoring investments. Don't overestimate what your offshore partner can accomplish. This is a process that will change as you become more experienced with offshoring.

- **Obtain corporate commitment.** Ensure that you have support from "C-level" executives (CEO, CIO, etc.) because offshoring may involve large labor displacements and business-process changes. There is no painless way to move toward a blended labor pool with the majority of resources residing in other countries. To execute a smooth transition for workers and contractors, focus on good human resources practices.

- **Don't assume less management will be needed.** Even if a third party will be handling the work day to day, long-term management of the provider will be necessary (even if the provider is an extension of the corporation). Look for professionals who have experience in managing a diverse set of remote resources. Certain workflow and software management tools can be helpful in managing this process. Budget extra time to accommodate time zone, language, and cultural differences.

SURVIVAL GUIDE
FOR BUYERS

- **Create and manage benchmarks.** Price is only one element of offshoring; quality, responsiveness, and productivity goals are critical as well. Healthy competition between offshore providers, domestic consultants, and in-house employees can provide insight as to the effectiveness and results of an offshore strategy. All offshore companies are not created equal; they have the same strengths and challenges as domestic service providers. Benchmark them in the same fashion.

SURVIVAL GUIDE
FOR SELLERS

OFFSHORING

Sellers should read the buyers' survival guide for ideas on how to better serve their markets. An additional set of considerations applies to sellers of these services:

- **Change your cost structure.** The market for services will remain strong, but not at current price points. Software is also undergoing price pressures. Expect that your services cost structure will have to be cut in the next three years by 30 to 50 percent. Understand how your service and R&D groups will need to be supplemented with offshore labor. Initial efforts should be through an established offshore provider, particularly one that has worked for other software companies.

- **Enhance service offerings.** Offshore providers will not (in the short term) be able to compete with domestic needs for process reengineering, enhancement, and best practices. To maintain current service margins, companies will have to add business expertise to their staff. Don't look to turn technologists into business experts—the skill sets vary widely. Add industry service personnel while offshoring technical service workers who don't have to deal with your customers.

CHAPTER EIGHT

CUTTING THE IT BUDGET DOWN TO SIZE

There's this bizarre notion in the computer industry that we'll never be a mature industry. [The industry] is as large as it's going to be.
—Larry Ellison, CEO, Oracle Corp.[1]

S OME PEOPLE MAY CONSIDER the idea of a contraction in total corporate technology spending to be ridiculous and naïve. But it is not. In hardware (both PCs and servers), the rate of price declines has overtaken the ability to expand the equipment's usage in corporations. According to market research company IDC, U.S. spending on IT hardware peaked at nearly $170 billion in 1999, dropped to $136 billion in 2001, and has been on a slight downward trail ever since.[2] The price of calls, bandwidth, and physical equipment has been on a steady decline for years, giving companies increased capabilities at lower prices.

The likely contraction in total technology consumption will be attributed not to any single element but rather to the culmination of multiple trends: offshoring, standard hardware, new technology approaches, pricing pressures, Microsoft, and others. Most companies will be able to significantly reduce their IT budgets if they choose to do so. The intelligent conclusion is that total IT spending could easily stay flat or even decline for years.

Spending drivers for information technology. IT departments spent much of the 1990s adding substantial costs and complexity to their companies. Over the next five to ten years, companies will deploy information technology on a better economic and operational footing with lower overall costs.

Spending driver	Cost trend	Future outcome
Offshoring/labor sourcing	Much lower	Between 30 and 70% of all people-related IT services will be offshored by 2010. An extreme focus will be placed on low-cost labor and transferable jobs.
Asset/inventory reduction	Lower to much lower	Review and rationalization of all IT assets will result in a onetime savings and ongoing lever for price reductions and asset consolidation.
IT pricing	Lower	Worldwide availability of less-expensive labor, software, and services will govern spending increases for most companies. Subscription-based sales models will lower risk and short-term costs for buyers. Sellers will realize lower initial revenue from buyers.
Open-source software	Lower	Major disruptive technology for installed software vendors. Buyers will use open-source as a pricing hammer, particularly for new projects. Basic software areas including operating systems, databases, and application servers will be first hit; eventually most software will be affected.
Hardware	Lower	PCs acting as Internet "dumb" terminals as well as increased utilization of servers will decrease the need to buy new equipment; maintenance, service costs will decrease for buyers.
Standard technology/ integration	Lower to flat	Mixed. The realization of web services and adoption of more standard technology may drive costs down, whereas the difficultly of executing them across a large and diverse asset base and programs will minimize gains.

(continued on next page)

Spending drivers for information technology *(continued)*

Spending driver	Cost trend	Future outcome
Microsoft	Lower to flat	Microsoft has a mixed impact on costs depending on which technology is used and the type of task.
ROI	Lower to flat	Mixed. Better operational focus and understanding of the impact of information technology will gradually permit companies to obtain better ROI.
New technologies, improvements	Flat	Because of experimentation, gains obtained by using new technologies are often counterbalanced against losses resulting from poor use. In the 1990s, new technologies drove spending much higher. The quick purchase of new technologies will be governed in the coming decade.
Legacy technology	Flat	Little will change for ongoing maintenance and upgrading of systems, although certain drivers and management techniques can keep costs down.
New business initiatives/processes	Higher	Companies will always turn to innovative technologies or uses to better themselves. This behavior increases IT spending but presumably delivers business benefits.
Government requirements	Higher	Increased government requirements (e.g., financial, environmental, export) will add to the IT burden without necessarily helping companies slash costs or increase revenues.
Competitive offerings	Higher to much higher	Spending money on technology will always be necessary to maintain certain aspects of business parity with competitors.
Next New IT Thing	Much higher (typically)	Innovations like the Web, along with perceived necessities like preparing for Y2K, drive spending to unnatural levels. Current levels of IT spending make it difficult for a Next New Thing to be realized.

The above table summarizes many of the key spending drivers for information technology, their cost implications, and their likely impact on the future of IT spending. For most companies, the drivers that slow spending over the next few years will overshadow those that increase spending. Regardless, most companies are now looking at a budget process that "robs Peter to pay Paul;" if a new spending driver is identified, it must be funded from existing resources. This situation is in sharp contrast to the 1990s, when many IT groups and organizations increased their budgets dramatically with every new business, technology, or government initiative. Combined, these trends will permit companies to turn their IT budgets around without a loss of service or capabilities.

CONTINUED TECHNOLOGICAL INNOVATION

These changes do not stop or reduce the need for innovative and productive use of technologies. For many companies, cost reductions in labor, hardware, and software will fuel the new technology-enabled business initiatives of the future. Some of these deployments include:

- **New initiatives.** When linked to business objectives and goals, IT can powerfully improve the competitiveness of a company. Corporations will always need new business initiatives requiring different types of IT, just as new machines are needed when old ones wear out. Such initiatives include demand management, which helps companies better predict sales and customer demand; automation of service/repair operations, which lowers the cost of labor and capital used to service equipment; and revenue enhancement, which helps companies determine optimal strategies to increase sales. However, these initiatives will not be funded or mismanaged as they were in the past. A greater focus on ROI, incremental technology deployments, and operational discipline will help IT expenditures translate to business success.

- **Regulations.** Government regulations will continue to force companies to respond with technologically oriented solutions. Several types of initiatives are intermittently forced upon companies, such as Sarbanes-Oxley[3] regulations, which create rules around managing financial records; Food & Drug Administration (FDA) regulations, which create rules around product traceability and manufacturing; and international-trade regulations, which create rules around the import and export of goods. Companies must comply or face onerous fees and/or criminal charges.

- **Customer service/competitive offerings.** Technologically facilitated product and service offerings will continue to be attractive to businesses. These offerings can create a competitive advantage or match what competitors already offer. For example, the need to operate a web site, track goods on the Web, deliver corporate information, or offer self-service capabilities often does little for productivity or market share (unless done preemptively), but such offerings are ongoing costs of staying competitive. On the other hand, using technology to custom-fit clothing over the Web, as Land's End does, can create a competitive advantage.

- **The Next New Thing.** IT spending often expands in reaction to the Next New Thing in technology. Fads come and go, but they consume lots of corporate money in the process, with questionable returns. It may be a while before buyers spend money as easily as they did in the 1990s, but such free spending may happen again once corporate memory (and write-offs) fades.

I believe companies have only scratched the surface of business improvements possible through the appropriate use of technology. Companies have many IT-enabled opportunities to increase their competitiveness, customer satisfaction, and profitability. The key to realizing these opportunities, however, will be a fundamentally different approach in buying and executing IT. Aggressive cost-cutting rather than aggressive spending and a higher standard of cost-to-benefit analysis will be the order of the day.

COST-CUTTING MEASURES

In nearly every survey of CIOs over the past few years, cost cutting has been one of the top concerns. "We sell in a cost-competitive area," said Doug, a CIO in high-tech manufacturing. "The days of big budgets without justification are over. We will be slashing our budgets drastically." Doug expects his budget to be slashed by 40 to

50 percent between 2002 and 2005 while he expects company growth to be up 10 percent per year during that period.

A poor economic climate has contributed to this reality, but a chronic lack of financial analysis for individual projects (or the entire IT budget) is equally to blame. Few companies conduct any type of regular financial analysis or ROI justification for ongoing projects that consume large portions of an IT budget.

For technologists, this situation represents a catch-22: If they have successfully implemented an IT project but it is not adopted broadly or well used, how many resources should be dedicated to its upkeep and maintenance? For example, one client spent more than $1 million on a customer service solution, successfully implemented it, and is paying over $100,000 annually in maintenance fees. Yet the business unit that decided to invest in the solution is using only a fraction of the solution capabilities, and those capabilities could be replaced by technology that already exists within the company. The initial scope of use changed, and so did the financial benefit. The IT group, however, must continue to maintain this costly solution.

This example is indicative of the challenges many IT groups face. They have implemented and maintained successive business initiatives for years and continue to do so even when these business initiatives fall into disuse. But rarely do business managers look to inventory or write off the technological portions of minimally used programs. Rapid changes in business management and strategies accentuate this problem.

A variety of studies have been released stating that IT groups are woefully ill-prepared to justify their expenditures.[4] Such behavior is not singular to corporations. A recent GAO study found that the U.S. Department of Defense has wasted more than $1 billion through the continued use and mismanagement of redundant IT systems.[5] These studies have facilitated the views that IT is either wasteful or being executed in a wasteful fashion. Either view is too simplistic.

Hindsight shows that although the spending initiatives were not misplaced, the amount of IT spending was. Today, the corporate challenge is to bring IT spending and benefits back into balance. "We spent so much time and money getting the initial implementation to work, we forgot how much capability the system really had," said Joyce, a client in the banking industry. "I don't think we'll need to spend much over the next few years as we continue to mine gems from our systems. Besides, we have lots of excess capacity that we can also use." IT groups by themselves cannot fix this imbalance. Business units must take responsibility for IT-related costs and the benefits derived (or not).

Balancing the IT budget

No two IT budgets are alike. The main categories of spending are hardware, software, services, and internal labor costs. Each of these categories includes different savings drivers that depend on the mix of technologies and how different rationalization, consolidation, and redeployment techniques are used.

As the table below illustrates, companies can reduce their IT budgets in different ways, depending on the size of the company, the range of solutions, and how the solutions are used. Technologists can use all these factors to reduce the cost of the services they offer. Business units can also look at these factors as a way to encourage IT organizations to monitor their costs. At the very least, buyers can use these factors as a bargaining lever against the existing base of suppliers. A systematic review of the technologies supported and the aforementioned factors will help companies understand the magnitude of potential cost reductions.

Spending cutbacks. Current trends in technology will decrease rather than increase IT budgets. Depending on their current spending profile, companies will be able to cut between 10 and 60 percent of their costs in different IT spending areas over a period of years.

Technology	Factors driving costs down	Potential savings
Hardware	Microsoft, Linux, Intel-based processors, consolidation, increased utilization	10–40%
Software	Open source, Microsoft, subscription-based pricing, increased competition, building internally, renegotiating licenses based on use	20–35%
Labor/internal costs	Supply of technologists, offshoring, automating technologies (e.g., voice recognition)	30–50%
Services	Offshoring, strategic sourcing	30–50%

Back to basics: responsible spending

Many companies are reexamining how they use and buy information technology. The Next New Thing in IT is fostering an enhanced operational focus and a new vision of how resources should be deployed.

To get an idea of how companies will change their view of IT spending, consider the case of Verizon Communications. Between 2000 and 2002, Verizon cut its IT staff by 20 percent and its outside vendor costs by 30 percent. Since 2000, it has cut its IT budget to 4 percent of sales from a telecom industry average of 6 percent.[6] Verizon's CIO, Shaygan Kheradpir, has aggressively cut costs in all areas by reviewing all areas of spending and not accepting IT organizational status quo, as shown in the table below.

Merrill Lynch, whose IT budget is larger than the GDP of nearly 60 nations, has also dramatically pared its IT budget. Marvin Balliet, former CFO for global technology and services and now first vice president of Merrill Lynch's Global Private Client Group technology prioritization process, said, "In 2003, technology spending will be less than it was in 1998 and down more than a third from the peak of 2000." This reduction is due to an operational discipline that was forced by a changing business and revenue model.

At one time, Merrill Lynch had more than 100 projects going that cost more than $2.5 million each. "Before, with technology projects, Merrill Lynch would always go platinum.... Now in many

Technology spending cuts at Verizon. Verizon has aggressively cut fat from its IT budget. Its relentless focus on budget and asset utilization is indicative of what many other companies will practice in the future. *Source: Wall Street Journal.*

Item	Savings
Server hardware	$100 million (45%)
Internal employees	20% cut in staff
External services	30% cut in cost
Global sourcing	$14 million (2002); $50 million (2003)
Storage	$3.5 million (storage utilization increased to 60%)
2002 IT budget	20% total cost reduction in 24 months

instances we go gold or silver, and everything continues to run fine," said Balliet. Merrill Lynch has been able to cut costs by putting the business units in charge of most IT expenditures.

In the late 1990s, IT groups frequently told business units how technology should be used. In 1999, two-thirds of Merrill Lynch's IT costs appeared as indirect charges to businesses. As a result, the businesses had little understanding of what their IT charges represented and were unable to manage their technology expenses.

Merrill Lynch realized this was a poor way to use and manage technology. So, it refocused its efforts by having business groups manage their technology expenditures as part of their operational budget. The IT group now reports to the business units. At the same time, the business groups were tasked with determining how technology would be used. The role of the IT group went from innovator/sponsor to advisor/executer.

In 2003, the business units managed 75 percent of the IT budget. These units are partnering with the IT groups to drive technology efficiency. When large IT projects are being deployed, the business units set up three-month project review cycles to determine if the project still has business value. If it doesn't, the project is halted with no detriment to the IT group.

Efforts by companies such as Verizon and Merrill Lynch are cutting the baseline costs of information technology with no decrease in effectiveness or use. Such efforts are good news for buyers but not for most sellers of technology.

IT SALES SLOW

If companies follow the examples of Merrill Lynch, Motorola, Verizon, and others, reduced IT spending is likely to have long-term consequences on the growth and health of companies that sell information technology. For them, the time when companies easily committed to millions of dollars of technology spending is paradise lost. Buyers are seeking shorter-term technology commitments and smaller up-front payments. A recent survey of software selling prices provides a rough sense of this change.

According to a 2003 survey taken at the Sand Hill Group's annual Enterprise conference, 55 percent of attendees stated that the average selling price of their software was between $100,000 and $500,000; 16 percent stated that it was from $500,000 to $1 million. Attendees said that more and more sales were falling at the lower end of these price ranges. In prior years, the prices estimated were toward the higher end of these ranges.[7]

As companies scale back IT spending and ration their resources, technology and related service providers will suffer revenue loss. Sellers need to prepare for the following:

- **Lower hardware sales.** Hardware vendors have already seen the impact of commodity pricing and vendor shakeouts. Their revenues have been flat for years. Current trends indicate that the revenue outlook in the short to medium term could continue or worsen if companies focus on obtaining better utilization from existing hardware systems as well as extending the lifetime of PCs. Hardware for Linux- and Windows-based servers is used for less than 15 percent of its capacity in many organizations. This is in contrast to 25 to 40 percent utilization for Unix-based systems and utilization greater than 60 percent for mainframe solutions. As PCs revert to terminals because of the Internet, their useful life will increase from four years to six or more.

- **Varied losses in all software sales categories.** Software vendors will be hit across the board. License fees will be forced down due to a combination of factors: Microsoft, subscription-based pricing, open source, and less expensive labor combined with better software tools. Service and maintenance fees—an increasingly large portion of software company revenue—will be pushed down as offshore providers offer similar services. In addition, as users inventory their IT assets and find many unused and underutilized licenses, software vendors will be forced to renegotiate maintenance and license contracts to maintain goodwill.

- **More competitive pricing for service providers and consultants.** Service providers and consultants will need to decrease their margins and operating expenses to offer companies a blended (domestic and offshore) software rate of no more than $80 per hour. The better ones will be able to stay profitable, but not without a reconfiguration of their global staff and a general decline in IT rates and salaries.

- **Renegotiations (downward) with current customers.** Buyers with tougher bargaining skills will increasingly squeeze large, incumbent vendors of both hardware and software products. Buyers will renegotiate current contracts, both license and maintenance, as a lever for future sales. Lower-priced options in the market will force sellers to renegotiate and lower their margins to maintain client satisfaction and customer mind share.

- **Niche vendors grabbing the loose change.** Smaller, newer vendors with unique capabilities will be partially immune to the problems facing incumbent sellers of information technology. If their products and technologies can be positioned to solve difficult problems that have a strong relationship to business results, then they will be able to acquire the few discretionary dollars business units have for such solutions.

The future of IT spending

Given these changes, technology sellers will be fighting for every available buyer dollar. However, most market research firms predict that once the economy improves, IT spending growth will exceed 5 percent per year. If past history holds true, this is a fairly safe prediction.

But as stated before, there is significant evidence that history will be a poor indicator of future spending. Much of what has happened for the last 30 years with hardware is positioned to occur with software, external services, and internal labor. This trend probably will not last 30 years or more, but it will last long enough to significantly decrease spending on IT and establish a new baseline before growth begins again. During this time, buyers will learn how to use technology more efficiently.

Through the economic downturn of 2000–2003, total spending on IT has been relatively flat. If the traditional view of IT spending growth proves true (provided the economy gets better with a GDP growth of 3 percent or more), spending should increase at a pace of 5 to 6 percent per year, leading to total spending of nearly $1.1 billion by 2007. Many market forecasters agree, as the chart below shows.

These projections, however, do not take into account any of the factors that allow companies to cut back on spending. The traditional view of IT assumes that nothing will change in the overall spending behavior of buyers and that nothing has changed in the pricing behavior of sellers. The traditional view asserts that the IT spending slowdown of 2000–2003 was merely an economic aberration that will resolve itself once the economy picks up. Given all the factors that have been mentioned in previous chapters, these assumptions are difficult to accept. Instead, we are seeing the beginning of a new era of flat or declining spending based on a broadly accepted new dogma on IT spending: Spend less to get more.

There are three potential "paradise lost" spending trends in addition to common wisdom. The first potential trend examines the conditions needed to realize flat spending in IT over the next few years. The next view charts a moderate 3 percent annual decline through 2007. The last, aggressive view predicts a 6 percent decline. Using these numbers, the total spending in 2007 would be $860

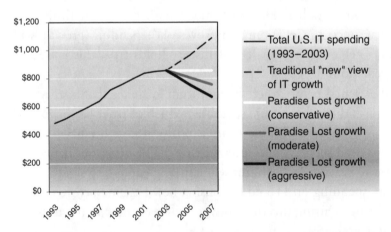

IT spending in the United States (in $ billions). Total spending for IT in the U.S. has been flat for the past few years.[8] There are four divergent scenarios for its growth over the next five years. Most market research firms are predicting a growth of 5 percent or more once the economy turns around. It is more likely that spending will be flat or drop.

billion, $760 billion, or $670 billion, respectively. There is a difference of nearly $450 billion between the prediction based on conventional wisdom and that based on aggressive user rationing and management of IT. It is instructive to examine the conditions by which alternatives to conventional wisdom become unavoidable.

Rules for flat spending

If spending remains flat through 2007, it will imply that companies as a group are acting much the same as in 2002 and 2003. Companies will look to minimize new IT purchases, seeing IT as a tactical tool and keeping much of their technology base at a status quo. New projects will be funded mostly through cuts in existing programs. New projects funded through business units will require rigorous ROI review. Selective offshoring and outsourcing will occur, as well as an increased focus on operational excellence. There will be continued price pressures on consultants.

Impact within IT organizations will be minimal, with little new hiring—attrition will take care of the cuts in staff necessary to keep budgets flat. A slow shift to offshored development will occur, with maintenance and tactical projects being the first to go. The remaining staff will be pressured to keep expenses flat, and a series of tactical cutbacks and hardware consolidations will probably occur every year. In addition, upgrade cycles will be slowed.

Keeping IT spending flat represents the simplest and least disruptive way to respond to past years of buildup and excess. IT and business groups can make positive changes to their use and effectiveness of IT resources if they do so slowly, deliberately, and with minimal disruption. Companies should be able to execute such a strategy with existing resources and personnel.

Rules for 3 percent spending cuts

A 3 percent annual spending cut on information technology will imply that companies are taking harsher measures, because total industry spending will decline by approximately 11 percent by 2007 within a growing economy. This type of spending implies a much more thorough review of all IT spending and operations. Companies will use their IT equipment—ranging from PCs to corporate servers to network routers—to maximum capacity and lifecycle. IT groups will run in conjunction with business-unit needs to ensure the prudence of new expenditures. Incremental spending will continue but will require a fairly rigorous ROI analysis. All offshoring options will be weighed, and many companies will elect to place a great deal of technical call center support and programming work offshore. Tactical use of domestic consultants will continue.

The impact within IT organizations will be large, because all aspects of operations and jobs will be reviewed for potential offshoring. Base programming and maintenance jobs will be under the most pressure, as will operational jobs running data and applications centers, because of their utility status. IT organizations will need to show increased productivity each year by taking on more operational duties and jobs at a lower cost. These organizations will also need to manage their IT assets intelligently.

Decreasing spending while running a growing business would tax any organization. Looking for constant cuts requires strong leadership from both IT and business managers. Employees with strong operational backgrounds will be needed to manage this effort. The ability to restrain and reduce budgets for years to come will require not only a strong synergy between IT and business groups but also staff changes, because some employees will be unable to make the transition effectively.

Rules for the biggest cuts

A 6 percent annual spending cut implies that companies will be taking hard, brutal cost-control measures, because total industry spending will decrease more than 20 percent by 2007. This type of contraction implies that IT operations will be extensively reviewed and every expenditure will be rationalized and put through an ROI exercise. The operational excellence of IT will need to match that of the best units of today's shrewdest companies by delivering a given level of service or capability at a lower cost every year.

Companies embarking on this type of cost-cutting requirement will review all assets and, through a total lifecycle management review, understand what should be cut and replaced with more optimal technology. Business units will take full responsibility for IT costs, and IT will be viewed as a key support for business operations. The maximum amount of IT will be offshored either through a third party or by companies setting up their own groups in low-cost, high-quality nations and venues. Use of domestic consultants will be extremely limited, unless their rates drop significantly from 2001–2003 pricing levels.

The impact within IT organizations will be considerable, because staffing requirements will change drastically. Remaining programmers will need to either supplement their skills with significant domain or customer expertise or have technical skills that are not readily available on the open market. IT organizations will shrink, or their jobs will be expanded tremendously to incorporate higher levels of skills and capabilities within the groups. Knowing how to effectively change business processes and obtain acceptance of newly deployed technology will also be key.

Such declines may seem counterintuitive or impossible, but leading companies have shown that they can easily decrease their total IT spending by more than 30 percent. A few have even been able to identify nearly 50 percent of their IT costs as expendable. This discovery is quickly becoming well known, so few companies will tolerate excessive budgets any longer. Managing IT for operational excellence will become *the* new requirement for many companies.

Clearly, this approach is one of the most disruptive paths that a company can attempt. Business units will be responsible for the success and use of a given technology within the corporation as well as managing its costs on a profit/loss basis. Companies will probably need to introduce new management personnel with a firm grasp of both technology and organizational skills. IT and business groups will work hand in hand with IT, focusing only on delivering the highest levels of service at a declining cost.

NOT ALL COMPANIES WILL TAKE THE JOURNEY

Some companies will dismiss such paths as imprudent or impossible. Although companies now have the opportunity to make cuts of 30 percent or more, we can expect less than a 6 percent and, more likely, less than a 3 percent annual decline in total spending for the next few years. This is the collective, slow-moving nature of companies. There will always be those that will not change their spending habits. A large difference exists between the potential cuts and those that will be realized. In addition, during the next few years an economic recovery will probably lull certain companies into falling back into their old spending habits. At the end of 2003, it appeared that U.S. buyers were ready to jump into yet another PC upgrade spending binge. Large vendors such as Microsoft will heavily market the need to upgrade to the latest versions of their respective wares. (It has always been easy to find reasons to spend more on IT.)

Companies today have a clear choice: They can continue their status-quo spending or embrace a new way of doing IT. Those companies that make the sweeping changes necessary to become better users of IT will put themselves in a vastly superior position, lowering the cost of technology while gaining better use from it. Those companies will have the opportunity to redefine their markets and competition.

In the next chapter, we will look into the logical future of IT spending and examine four alternative strategies and their predictable outcomes.

CHAPTER NINE

THE FOUR PATHS
OF IT SPENDING

In order to enter into a state where there is no desire and no suffering, one must follow a certain path.... Following the Noble Path is like entering a dark room with a light in hand; the darkness will all be cleared away and the room will be filled with light.

—The Teaching of Buddha,
Society for the Promotion of Buddhism[1]

A S COMPANIES LOOK to new and more prudent IT spending strategies, they need to decide not only how *much* they will spend on IT but also *what* they will spend that money on. IT spending follows one of four distinctive paths. In this and the chapter that follows, we explore these paths and how companies must change their direction to take advantage of the new spending trends in IT.

THE FOUR PATHS OF SPENDING

As discussed in previous chapters, companies can assess their technology use by comparing how much they spend on technology with the business benefits that result. The total amount spent includes capital expenditures, salaries, consultant fees, and similar expenses. It is a number that can be easily calculated—these items are simply added up.

The business benefits derived from technology are *not* as easy to determine. There are two ways to approach this comparison: the theoretical (our strategy, or what we believe will happen) and the actual (the business result of spending, or what really does happen). The theoretical is the number (or benefit) that is used when a technology is initially proposed or purchased. For example, say Acme Corp. decides to spend $1 million on a new technology because it believes that, once implemented, the technology will permit the company to lower its cost of processing a customer order by 30 percent. That is the *theory*. The actual *benefit* (as well as total spending) could be higher (or lower) than this projection once the system is implemented and in use.

The actual business benefit (lowering the cost of processing a customer order) can be determined only after the project has been implemented successfully. Acme can take before-and-after measurements to determine this benefit. It can also examine total spending (initial and ongoing) to determine what it actually spent on the program. At that point, Acme can evaluate the advantages the technology brought to the company relative to the money spent on the project. Acme should continue taking measurements to ensure that benefits continue every year the technology is used.

Once we ascertain the technology spending levels in any given company, we can determine its IT buying strategy or approach. By examining the business benefits and pitfalls of those strategies, we can see how well these strategies are used or executed. Together, these two measurements determine the path of IT spending a company has taken. These paths, however, vary greatly; companies can follow many trajectories.

To illustrate this point, let's say we are sitting on top of a donkey with a mind of its own. We have purchased the donkey for a considerable sum of money to do various chores, and right now we want to use the donkey for transportation. But the donkey won't move. We assumed that it would be a simple matter to get the donkey to go from one location to another, but it is not so easy.

A number of strategies are available to us to get the donkey moving. We learn from the seller that a clicking sound encourages him to move. We could also tap the donkey with a stick, tempt it with a carrot, or pull it along. Each strategy will have a different effect on where and how far the donkey goes. Until we reach our final destination, however, we can only estimate the transportation effectiveness of our donkey, based on our past knowledge or assumptions. Some strategies will make the donkey go to our desired destination in an expeditious and direct manner; others will make the donkey take a slow and painful route. Ultimately, we may decide that we need to buy another donkey or a horse (or even a car!) to reach our destination.

While most technologies are more dependable than a donkey, the business benefits received by corporations have a similar degree of inconsistency. Most technology solutions appear to have a mind of their own, though in fact they perform only as told (or programmed). This confusion is due to our inability to predict how any complex technology really works when combined with people and existing systems. Corporations are all looking to go to a similar destination, but they wind up shooting off in different directions and never reaching their destinations. For IT buyers, these directions can be sorted into one of four styles of corporate spending:

- **The Path of Propaganda**—Buying what the sellers tell them to buy
- **The Path of Problems**—Using high-spending strategies from the past
- **The Path of Pennies**—Buying the bare minimum of software and hardware on the market
- **The Path of Profits**—Balancing price and productivity carefully

As shown in the figure on the following page, once the decision is made and the direction determined, companies embark on one of the four spending paths—for better or worse.

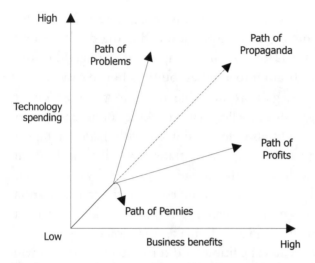

The four styles of corporate IT spending. Corporations can take four very different paths with their IT investments. Unfortunately, most companies divide their spending characteristics between the Path of Pennies and the Path of Problems. Few take the Path of Profits. The Path of Propaganda is the difficult, theoretical path that sellers tell us is right around the corner but that few ever realize.

The Path of Propaganda

This path translates into myriad claims of "when you install xyz technology, you can realize a positive ROI in six months or less." This path is promoted by sellers of technology with a vested self-interest. The Path of Propaganda promises that high IT spending will translate into extraordinary business benefits. This propaganda is promulgated by nearly every interested party in the IT industry. Vendors, industry analysts (both Wall Street and technical), user groups, and others promote this message for an obvious reason: money.

Industry-spending averages collected and promoted by various groups are one of the most dangerous metrics used to promote this path. While there is nothing inherently wrong with these numbers, they imply that if a company is spending less on technology than its peers, that company is at a strategic disadvantage.

As discussed in chapter 4, this has become one of the big lies of the IT industry. The few companies that are on this path (many of which are in the pharmaceutical and financial services industries) typically spend slightly more on IT than the average firm and have a wide array of custom packages installed. These companies pay a lot for technology and enjoy a fair-to-good business benefit, but at a higher cost than is necessary.

The Path of Propaganda may be considered ideal, but it is also rarely realized. Typically, companies veer away from it because spending more on technology overrides budgetary concerns. This extra spending quickly adds up. It is an expensive path that is difficult to take, particularly for those industries with low margins and that are unable to raise prices easily. Only companies in industries with fairly high margins—where IT costs can be buried or marginalized—are able to remain on this spending tightrope. Most do not, and instead find themselves on the following path.

The Path of Problems

Many companies, such as FoxMeyer, have found themselves on the Path of Problems after a decade of unrestrained spending. Just as the road to hell is paved with the best intentions, so is the Path of Problems. Companies on this path made investments that they believed were prudent. They gambled large financial resources on the potential positive outcome of their technology expenditures. And they wasted a great deal of money.

A variety of factors lead unsuspecting companies down this path. Such companies often have poor project and technology management. When a project falls behind schedule, they throw more money at it, often with poor results. Projects that fall within budget often deploy only a fraction of what was initially projected. The intended ROI is never achieved (and not even measured) once the project is completed.

Companies on the Path of Problems have a wide array of technologies—both advanced and simple—but effectively use only a portion of them. More than a few are used counterproductively. Expensive supply chain packages sit unused because they are too complex for planners. Sales employees do not use CRM packages because it is easier to close business deals without them.

The Path of Problems is common for many companies. None of the difficult issues of getting technology to deliver a business benefit are addressed up front. Instead, when these companies implement projects, their attention is focused on the benefits of completing a project. But even when a project is completed on time and on budget, it is considered a failure because it is not used within the corporation as planned. (Note: This is the road less traveled in Europe, where companies tend to be much more introspective about their IT investments. In general, Europeans spend less on technology—as a percentage of GDP—than their North American counterparts.[2])

This path and its associated problems are leading many companies (and a few prognosticators) to go to the other extreme, suggesting that companies focus only on the cost of IT and follow the Path of Pennies.

The Path of Pennies

The Path of Pennies is being taken increasingly by major companies. These companies have come to one of two conclusions. The first is that they have spent too much on technology and see great opportunities for cost reduction. Motorola (profiled in chapter 5) is one such company. The second conclusion is that technology is a simple commodity and should be considered a tactical cost of doing business and thus kept to a minimum. Companies that come to the second conclusion focus on the pennies of IT and look at the little picture (cost) rather than the big picture (how IT can become a powerful strategic tool). These companies often purchase the least expensive products and attempt to stretch out their life as long as possible—with only a minimal payback. The only advantage that they have over others is that they have not "wasted" excessive monies on IT failures.

Given the averages for IT success, this path may not be a bad one to take. Depending on the industry, this approach follows a similar path taken by index-based financial investors: If you assume that you cannot beat the averages, then it is better to invest an average amount (or, in the case of IT spending, less than average).

Such a view makes these companies consider spending averages as something to beat by a wide margin. They will always come in below the average regardless of the purpose of the expenditure. There is little synergy with business units, and IT is charged to the company much like electricity, telephone, or janitorial services. The focus is to cut this cost every year.

This path was promoted by Nicholas Carr in his May 2003 *Harvard Business Review* article, "IT Doesn't Matter," where he stated that IT can no longer garner any distinct business advantages because it has become a commodity. He concluded that IT should be managed down to the lowest possible level. Although many with a vested interest in IT have disputed his view, it may be the path to take for a few companies as well as a temporary path for big spenders. We will explore the characteristics of such companies in the next chapter.

As a former client proved, however, there is a big difference between being frugal and being cheap.

A number of years ago, Bill called with his CEO George on the line. Bill was the CIO of a $600 million custom machinery company based in the Midwest. After spending months selecting a product for Bill's company, we had determined that Symix (an ERP software company that has since been renamed Frontstep and acquired by MAPICS) met the company's needs. We had been able to negotiate a 27 percent discount, which was good, given the size of the deal. This was the final phone call to go over some contract details, or so I thought. George was first to speak.

"What is the COGS [cost of goods sold] for software?"

This was a strange question. Why was it coming up now? "Could you explain what you are looking for, George?" I asked.

"It's simple," he said. "This software seems pretty expensive, and I want to know what the COGS are for software."

"For most companies it is pretty small. You are talking about the cost of the media and a few other things. In the software business, gross margins are usually north of 85 percent."

George came back: "Then why am I paying so much? My gross margins are nowhere near that high."

"Well, it's for all the cost associated with software. The vendors have a lot of domain knowledge that is part of a high R&D expense. They needed to fly teams of people out to your site for the evaluation process. Many costs are associated with selling software, so while COGS is low, expenses surrounding the entire exercise of selling this type of software are high."

George was not buying it, and Bill was getting worried. "I know that I need to buy this type of software now, but the cost seems excessive. Perhaps we should be considering alternatives." After the call, Bill told me what had happened.

At the eleventh hour, a competitive company (one that had initially been taken out of consideration because its software was not Y2K compliant) came back to my client's CEO with a sweet deal. It said that it would give its software to my client for free with the provision that it would perform all services (e.g., installing, maintaining, customizing) on a time-and-materials basis. The proposed contract difference was $100,000 on a $400,000 deal. The company assured my client that future upgrades of its software would be Y2K compliant. George liked this and decided to override Bill and go with the alternative instead. Unfortunately, nine months and $100,000 over budget later, my client had to scrap its installation, patch its old system for Y2K fixes, and look for a different package. Cheap can cost. Sometimes, the Path of Pennies can be the most expensive path of all.

The Path of Profits

The final and most difficult path of all is the Path of Profits. Those who attempt this path—companies such as Harrah's and JetBlue Airways—realize that there is not much of a relationship between technology spending and business benefits. They know that to gain a return on any IT investment, a tight link with businesses and a relentless focus on what will be obtained by any given expenditure is required. These companies invest heavily, but not excessively, on technologies that support their business needs. Their business greatly profits from the use of technology and its incorporation into their business strategy.

The strategy varies by the type of company. For example, Dell—which is strong in low-cost products—focuses on procurement and sourcing functions where it will extract the best possible price from its subcontractors. On the other hand, companies with a strong market share and a talent for exploiting their current customer base, such as Harrah's, focus on marketing and customer-facing investments.

The companies that take the Path of Profits follow a rigorous process, measuring and managing every IT investment regardless of type. IT investments are made with business units, which take responsibility for the success or failure of projects. Because of this focus on results and project management, there is not much wasteful IT spending or excess within the corporation.

Like those on the Path of Propaganda or Problems, these companies are looking for strong business benefits. They believe that technology can provide a differentiating element to their business strategy. Like those on the Path of Pennies, they are looking to get more from every dollar they spend on IT and aim to cut their IT costs every year, as they do other operational costs.

To obtain these seemingly diverse objectives, they juxtapose their business creativity with operational IT rigor. They are cautious with the amount of money they spend on IT but aggressive with how they use it. They look to reduce their baseline and ongoing costs

Companies take one of four paths for IT spending. The behaviors and spending characteristics help to identify where companies belong in this model.

Path of IT spending	IT peer spending characteristic	Characteristic behavior	Examples
Problems	Average to higher than average	IT deployed for itself and business; aggressive spending without strong business benefit correlation; poor cost oversight and project management	FoxMeyer, Hershey (during its 1990s ERP implementation), Nike (during its 2000 SCM implementation)
Propaganda	Higher than average to average	Same as Problems but with better business results and links to business units	Pharmaceutical, financial services, technology industries
Profits	Lower than average	IT as cost and profit center with tight business sponsors, strong project and cost management, as well as ROI metrics	Harrah's, JetBlue, Wal-Mart, Dell; retail, wholesale industries
Pennies	Lower to much lower than average	IT as cost center, no tie in with business, minimum spending, tight spending controls	Oil and gas industry

every year but will take these savings and reapply them to new projects. Their strategies represent a continuous circle of improvement powered by cycles of cost cutting. Their paths represent a sawtooth pattern of spending, with increases in strategic spending alternating with tactical cost reductions. It is definitely a hands-on process. The companies that take this path know how to take advantage of technology at the lowest possible cost.

The table on the previous page summarizes the ideas presented so far about the four paths. To understand the dynamics and management styles that are needed on the Path of Profits, let's take a look at two leaders: Harrah's and JetBlue.

Harrah's: on the Path of Profits

Harrah's, the largest and most profitable gaming company in the United States, is proof that technology can have a strong impact on a company. With more than $4 billion in revenues (not counting what is given to native tribes) and a $1.1 billion EBITDA (Earnings Before Interest, Taxes, Depreciation, and Amortization) in 2002, the Las Vegas, NV-based firm is one of the most admired companies in America. Technology is a key part of its strategy to dominate the gaming market and gain customer loyalty. Harrah's does this by breaking all the traditional IT rules:

- It spends less than 2 percent of revenue on technology, with an IT budget of only $70 million in 2003.
- It builds its own solutions for CRM, demand, and price optimization.
- It has integrated all customer information to make it valuable for marketing and operations people alike.
- It's in the process of integrating and networking every slot machine, gambling station, restaurant, and asset to create a customized decision support system.
- Every IT expenditure, including typical infrastructure expenditures, is expected to generate an ROI.

The business results of doing things the "Harrah's way" are impressive. Between 1998 and 2002, revenues more than doubled. Harrah's has increased its share of total customer spending on gambling, up to 43 percent (from 36 percent) between 1998 and 2002. Average daily gaming and hotel revenues per total available rooms increased from $153 to $229 between 2000 and 2002. But it wasn't always like this, according to John Boushy, senior vice president of operations, products, services, and IT.

"Ten years ago [in 1993] IT was viewed as a cost center and not strategic," Boushy said. "We [stretched] every dollar we spent on IT." At that time, Harrah's had revenues of $1 billion and spent 0.8 percent of that on technology—less than half its rate today.

In my years of talking with companies on their use of IT, I have rarely come across a company that has integrated its business strategy with its technology so well. Key to this success is the fact that in the mid-1990s, Harrah's started to align its IT and business organizations. Harrah's made the business group responsible for the success or failure of the integration and taught the IT groups how introducing new projects (and maintaining old ones) can influence the company's cash flow.

"In 2004, we will be adding $5 million to IT costs as a result of projects that we completed in 2003. We are expecting over $22 million of incremental profits [in 2004] from those investments. The entire discussion about IT is investment oriented, where the money should be coming from and where on the P&L sheet it will appear," said Boushy.

Much of Harrah's secret lies in the creation of a real-time custom CRM solution that permits it to manage each customer individually, according to a different profile. This profile includes the experience each customer is having at any Harrah's at any given point in time. This is accomplished through the use of membership cards that help the company track a customer's activities within its facilities. The cards are also tied to highly sophisticated demand management, pricing, and customer software that helps to optimize the Harrah's experience for the customer—and helps Harrah's manage corporate profits.

This system has allowed the company to better understand where its customers spend their gambling dollars, how much they spend, and how fast they spend it. "We treat everybody differently," according to Gary Loveman, Harrah's CEO. "God created all people equally. God did not create all customers equally.

"What has made us successful is a constant theme of simplification," added Loveman, explaining that all initiatives are focused on increasing brand recognition, increasing customer loyalty, and the strategic use of technology. This perspective changes the way that Harrah's looks at its properties and businesses. "We don't think of hotels as hotels. We think of them as places where gamblers sleep. We don't think of restaurants as restaurants. We think of them as a place where gamblers go to refuel."

To facilitate this approach, Harrah's created demand and pricing systems that reflect each customer's gambling expenditures. Room rates can vary by hundreds of dollars a night, depending on an individual's information in the company's database. Everything Harrah's does is focused on capturing a greater share of the annual gaming budget of its customers. And it works.

This simplification is not necessarily all technological. The technologies in use at Harrah's range from 2 to 20 years in age. "As soon as a system is implemented, it is legacy," said Boushy. "We are challenged by the different systems we have, so we focus on getting the information contained in all of them integrated into a single enterprise data warehouse and a single offering [order management] system."

Harrah's has a little of everything: various types of PCs; local area and wide area networks; IBM AS/400s, which are used for its hotels and casinos; Unix systems, which are employed for database applications; Unix and Windows NT servers, which are used for web applications; and its customer marketing/analysis database, which resides on a Teradata computer. While Harrah's is always looking to consolidate its computing systems, unless there is a real business benefit, systems are left alone. The company looks first at its business goals and then evaluates technology on an item-by-item basis to see whether it can create more profit.

Harrah's is a great example of the currently accepted view that there is no relationship between the amount of IT spending and business effectiveness. Just as we'd find in the gaming rooms at Harrah's, there are winners and losers at all spending levels. What matters most in poker is how well you play, and Harrah's has played the IT game better than most.

JetBlue: flying toward the Path of Profits

With JetBlue, a New York–based airline that hit revenues of more than $1 billion in less than three years of operation, it is a different story. JetBlue's goal is to be a low-cost provider in an industry that bleeds money. Like Southwest Airlines, it operates with a cost model that is 30 to 40 percent below that of traditional airlines and takes advantage of the latest technology to keep its costs low. For instance:

- With a single exception, JetBlue is a pure Microsoft shop, an approach that eliminates the high costs of integrating multiple systems.

- It uses Voice Over Internet Protocol (VOIP) technology to eliminate the need for a centralized call center, dramatically cutting call center costs.

- It equips its pilots with laptop computers that hold all the documentation needed for their flights, eliminating costly and sometimes out-of-date paper documents.

JetBlue's operating results illustrate that its goal of delivering excellent customer service at the lowest cost has been achieved. As of mid-2003, it had 10 consecutive quarters of profitability, with a 19 percent operating margin. Its on-time performance and airplane load factor place it consistently at the top. JetBlue's revenue growth continues to outpace expense growth. It does all of this on an IT budget (expenses and capital spending) of about $25 million (in 2003).

"We have advantages over our peers because of our lack of legacy systems and the simplicity of our business model," said Tim Claydon, senior vice president of sales and business development. "Given our simplified fare structure, the fact that we rely on a single type of aircraft, that we don't do cargo, and that we don't use travel agents, we do not need to make the type of [IT] investments that competitors do." (Note: This interview was conducted before JetBlue announced that to explore new markets, it would add a second type of aircraft with less capacity than its current Airbus planes.)

Recent internal analysis at JetBlue indicated that it is spending about the same amount on IT (as a percent of revenue) as other transportation vendors. The nature of the spending, however, is different. For instance, because it uses Internet technology to remotely deploy its reservation agents at their homes, it does not need to lease or construct a building to house employees. Although these employees are centered around Salt Lake City, JetBlue is expanding its wide area network capabilities in order to be less geographically limited.

One of the ways that JetBlue is able to keep its costs down is its strategic partnership with Microsoft, which permits it to simplify its IT structure and enjoy low licensing fees. "Microsoft has worked very hard with us to show that its technology can run the level of transactions that are needed," said Claydon. He added that JetBlue's reservation system, which is provided by a third-party supplier, is being rewritten in Microsoft-specific technology.

Using Microsoft as its key IT supplier doesn't mean that JetBlue has nothing to worry about. When its data center was first set up, it was populated with a dozen hardware servers in a single physical location. A few years of growth increased that to more than 250 servers at 3 data centers by the end of 2002. JetBlue saw this as a good opportunity to consolidate, and it did.[3] For example, Jetblue.com (the company's web site) grew from having 2 commodity Compaq servers to needing a total of 64 servers; it then replaced those 64 servers with 3 Unisys high-end servers to save on hardware and labor costs. Through the use of software from EMC Corp., storage utilization has been increased from 37 to 87 percent.

All of these decisions were made to keep costs down. JetBlue believes that a primarily Microsoft-specific environment is a key enabler of that. It needs to ensure high availability and response time for all its systems; over 70 percent of all tickets are booked over the Internet (JetBlue does not sell paper tickets). Its customer service agents (more than 750 in all) operate from their homes using VOIP technology. JetBlue also uses an interactive voice-response server to reduce the number of calls that must be handled physically by agents. The server prompts customers through a menu of choices and answers most calls without human intervention.

JetBlue also provides its pilots with laptop computers. Other airlines give their pilots huge paper documents that must be updated a few times every week. Such documents are cumbersome and heavy. JetBlue crafted an application that automatically updates the electronic versions of such documents every time a pilot logs into the

JetBlue network. This application saves each pilot an estimated 24 hours of work a year and saves the company more than 10,000 hours per year of worker time.

Using technology effectively is a key strategy of JetBlue. Offering a web-based reservation system, using wireless technology to assist customer check-in, and creating a custom-procurement application for its company store (for customers to buy JetBlue logo-ware) have all had a direct impact on keeping JetBlue's total costs down.

Claydon said that JetBlue's rapid growth now requires the company to reexamine its cost model for IT. He added that he believes he will be able to bring his IT cost below that of the average transportation company in the next year or so. The company has created a P&L (profits and loss) committee to review and better manage its IT investments.

"We will be very tight [on IT spending increases] in 2004. Our focus today is to enhance and invest in our technological infrastructure to ensure that it meets the performance needs of our customers [as the business continues to grow rapidly]," said Claydon. "IT is a great enabler, but we never lose sight that it is JetBlue's customer service that provides the value to customers."

Harrah's and JetBlue: spending differences

When we compare Harrah's and JetBlue, as illustrated in the next chart, on the surface the differences appear to be large—but, really, they are small. For example, JetBlue focuses on cost reduction, whereas Harrah's focuses on revenue generation. Given the industries in which they participate and the behavior of their customers, this makes perfect sense.

JetBlue is part of an industry in which an increasingly large segment of the customer base cares primarily about cost. If everything else is equal, then the low-cost ticket will get the customer almost every time. Anything that JetBlue's IT department can do to keep the cost per passenger mile down will enable it to charge less for travel than its competitors. If part of the cost reduction also helps to improve customer relations and the travel experience, then this is an added bonus.

Harrah's, on the other hand, participates in an industry in which the concept of customer loyalty has never been a major consideration. Customers are attracted to different gambling establishments via flashy new or updated facilities. Harrah's believes that if it better understands its customers' spending behavior and treats each customer as an individual, then it can attract more business. All of its IT investments are centered around this belief.

JetBlue applies IT at every step of the *airline* process (from making seat reservations to delivering passengers to their final destinations), thus making the customer experience no worse (and perhaps better) than its competitors. Harrah's applies IT at every step of the *gambling* process (from the room reservation to the casino visit to the trip back home) to make the total experience enjoyable for its customers.

Through different approaches to IT, each company has been able to achieve its goals.

"We are a leading practitioner in CRM, but not financial management [in areas such as procurement]," said Harrah's Boushy.

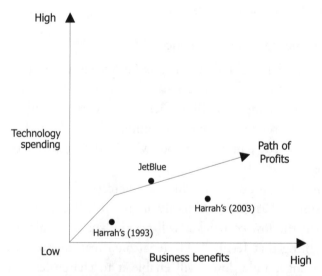

A comparison of Harrah's and JetBlue. They are focusing on different business challenges, but both are using technology strategically to get on the Path of Profits. JetBlue does this through business simplicity and a relentless focus on cost reduction; Harrah's looks to increase revenues through increased customer satisfaction. Over the last 10 years, Harrah's has moved to the Path of Profits from the Path of Pennies.

"There are many companies that do procurement much better than us. It's something we will eventually get to." JetBlue, which has been focusing on costs, is now building a customer database and analysis capabilities to complement its frequent-flyer program.

Both JetBlue and Harrah's rely on a great deal of custom software. They use standard types of packages, such as Microsoft Office and ERP software, for financial reporting and analysis. Unlike other companies, they have identified key differentiating business processes where IT can, and will, make a difference. Because these processes are often not well understood by peers, few software packages are available that can accommodate them. This forces the companies to build solutions rather than buy them.

Both companies have made minimal use of outside consulting firms to build their IT strategies. For JetBlue, not using consultants is an issue of cost: Using contractors is more expensive than using a well-managed internal staff. For Harrah's, not using consultants is an issue of experience: It wants to keep the domain expertise that it has developed. (Harrah's is currently looking at how it can use offshoring to decrease tactical IT deployment.)

Harrah's and JetBlue are at different points in their corporate lifecycle. Harrah's comes from a legacy of spending tactically and has moved into strategic use of IT while slowly increasing its expenditures. JetBlue is building everything from the ground up. For now, it will have a higher degree of spending than Harrah's because its efforts cannot be as well dispersed across a company of its size.

GETTING TO THE PATH OF PROFITS

JetBlue and Harrah's didn't just accidentally stumble upon the Path of Profits. Each combined a strategic technical vision with an understanding of business and operations. These two companies were able to jump on the path from different places: JetBlue as a start-up with a focus on low-cost airline tickets, Harrah's as a casino that underspent on technology for years. Both share one thing: a ruthless focus on lowering the cost of IT.

To join them on the journey to the Path of Profits, companies must focus on eliminating IT waste.

CHAPTER TEN

REACHING THE PATH
OF PROFITS

Some people skate to the puck. I skate to where the puck is going to be!
—Wayne Gretzky,
all-time leading scorer in professional hockey

M OST COMPANIES would like to be in the market-leading
position of JetBlue, Harrah's, Dell, or Wal-Mart. Information technology has helped them secure their respective spots in the sun. These companies have a relentless
goal to keep the cost of technology down and have combined the
best of IT and business leadership.

But it takes more than a simple handshake between groups to
start on the journey toward the Path of Profits: It requires operational discipline and a linkage between business and technology
units. Only recently have companies not on the Path of Profits followed the lead of their more successful counterparts who require
more operational discipline from their IT groups as well as more IT

participation from their business units. Bridging this gap is the single greatest breakthrough a company can make. For most Fortune 500 companies, effectively merging the entrenched mindsets of IT and business units would be a major step forward in corporate evolution.

Companies that master the art of finely tuned, cost-effective IT management will have a major advantage. Their success will force their competitors to also master the art or fail miserably. As discussed in chapter 4, this phenomenon has already occurred in the retail and wholesale distribution markets, which have had to react to Wal-Mart's IT mastery, not to mention its ruthless grab for market share and revenue growth. Other industries will follow. This trend will change not only the face of IT but the future of corporate America as well.

As world markets continue to open, the potential gains are greater than ever. But so are the potential losses. The future belongs to those who are perceptive enough to grasp the significance of what has happened to IT and resourceful enough to synchronize business management and information management.

SPEND LESS, GET MORE

The seeds for this change have been sown. Business weeklies and boardrooms are increasingly recognizing that companies do not need to spend a great deal of money on IT to obtain large business gains. Although the economy (and technology-based spending) slowed from 2000 to 2003, productivity gains continued to increase. In the second quarter of 2003, U.S. productivity was up 5.7 percent;[1] in the third quarter it was up an aberrant 9.4 percent. Companies were forced to do more with less, and they did.

Companies can no longer afford to jump reactively into every IT trend. The slowdown has allowed companies to better understand what they need, what they use, and what they can cut. As the economy improves, companies need to continue this discipline rather than fall back into old spendthrift ways. Those profligate ways do not lead to success anymore—in fact, they never did.

Cutbacks in technology spending should not be considered just a reaction to an economic downturn; rather, they are a starting point for a corporate opportunity to reach the Path of Profits as well as an

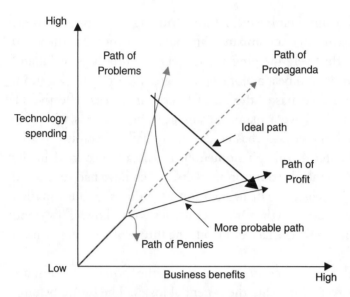

Getting to the Path of Profits. Many companies would love to take a beeline from the Path of Problems to the Path of Profits. However, few organizations can accomplish such a transformation. They should begin by lowering IT costs and then determine with the business groups how to better use technology.

opportunity to forge a much closer alliance between business and technology. By forging this linkage, companies can begin to consider which spending path to take in the future.

Once companies understand the issues and put a plan into place, they will move to the Path of Profits naturally. But it is a difficult journey that requires business leaders and management who not only believe the journey is worth taking but also have the skills to guide companies to that path confidently. History includes many more examples of business failures through the excessive use of badly implemented technology than business failures through the insufficient use of IT. Like high-stakes poker, there is no one formula for success: Too much or too little risk-taking can be equally hazardous.

Walking before running

The move to the Path of Profits often requires a stop at the Path of Pennies. Given the history of technology failures, companies need to first consider how to cut wasteful IT spending before tackling ways to better use existing technology, as the chart above shows. That is the path Motorola has taken, as discussed in chapter 5. Unfortunately, most companies are unable to move directly from the Path of Problems to the Path of Profits because of the following factors:

- **Lack of discipline.** Cutting IT budgets 20 percent or more while working on ways to better use existing systems is more than most organizations can handle. In trying to do both, companies usually wind up doing neither.

- **Lack of trust.** If IT and business groups have not been working well together because of all the changes that must be made, a crash program in "togetherness" often causes more collision than collaboration.

- **Lack of focus.** It has been said that 90 percent of a great athlete's performance is over before the starting gun. Invariably, any great feat of coordination takes much practice. The same is true with corporations; they need to practice business/IT baton handoffs until they are routine. Companies need to get their technology house in shape before launching remarkable strategic initiatives. They also need to get their business groups in sync with the possibilities of technology.

This last point was familiar to Harrah's Gary Loveman. When he joined the company in 1998 as COO, he saw that the company's web site was horrible. "I told my staff not to spend one cent on fixing it," said Loveman. "I told them to try to direct people away from it, as we had more important things to do." His business strategy was to use the Web intensively, but the back-end and customer-data systems needed would not be ready for 18 months. So Harrah's let the site sit. Once the back-end systems were ready, the site was rebuilt. Today, it is a significant driver of revenue for Harrah's.

Many organizations have a long way to go before the IT and business units can come together for a single purpose. But once they do, the results can be astounding.

CUTTING BACK

As stated in chapter 5, companies first need to know what they have before they try to cut back. Distributed buying and installations of technology cause many companies to underestimate what they have. "[In any cost reduction exercise] you need to create an industry standard language, get benchmarks, collect data, have your cost drivers defined, and link billings to these cost drivers," said Toby Redshaw, Motorola's corporate vice president of IT. "That gives you a line of sight between what you are charged and what you get. Then you get interested people [the business customers] and the smart guys who know how to cut costs."

Inventorying and reviewing all IT expenses is key to these processes, first by technologists and then by business leaders. "In most businesses, if you have a two-hour meeting with the head of your operations unit, that person will know 75 percent of their assets and cost drivers," said Redshaw. "It should be no different for technology. So for instance, in this plant I should have this ratio for desktops, computing power, networks, etc., and I know what the right number is."

When IT and business groups come together, the first order of business should be to better understand how well technology

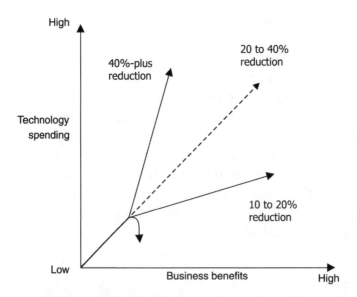

Potential IT spending reductions for companies. IT spending reductions are a function of where a company resides in its effective use of technology. Different expectations for cutbacks should be made depending on the installed base of technology and the nature of its use.

initiatives relate to business benefits. IT groups by themselves can cut costs (mostly operational) with insights such as which applications in the inventory are used, how well certain technologies work, and what a given piece of functionality is worth. When business groups are brought into the equation, more than 40 percent can sometimes be cut from an IT budget. The potential for savings is a function of IT business efficiency: The greater the inefficiency, the greater the ability to make cuts.

Once a company begins complaining about IT budget malaise, IT managers have several possible approaches to curing it, depending on the severity of the problem. When the cost-cutting pill is analyzed in terms of percentage of the IT budget, all remedies boil down to one of three categories: mild (10 to 20 percent), medium strength (20 to 40 percent), and extra strength (40 percent or more), as the chart on the previous page shows. The less painful the headache, the less painful the cure. Firms should not fool themselves into believing that there is no potential for more cost cutting. Leading companies try to cut operating costs every year and ruthlessly cull the budget for wasted resources. Even frugal companies have a potential for savings.

Mild medicine: the 10 to 20 percent solution

Companies that have followed the Path of Pennies or the Path of Profits often have little room to cut. These companies have done nearly everything they can to decrease spending. New projects are scrutinized carefully, and business groups take responsibility (often on a P&L basis) for the success or failure of the projects. Existing investments are combed to see where extra dollars can be had.

Companies that follow the Path of Pennies look only at cost issues—the cheaper the better. If they want to use technology more strategically, they may increase certain budget items, because their frugal way of using IT leaves them with little room for business benefits. Cuts in this range can often be executed with little input from business groups. Increased operational efficiencies, better terms and conditions on contracts, and a simple reexamination of labor are all ripe areas for reduction that can be handled from a purely technological basis. Even with focused spending, companies can look to trim budgets. Areas include the following:

- **Limited offshoring.** Even low-spending companies can derive benefits from offshoring. With the increasing ability to garner high-quality, low-cost resources abroad, there are providers that will take on small, short-term jobs and undercut regional consulting firms. Tactical and maintenance chores are the best to send to offshore providers, initially.

- **Strategic sourcing.** One area of IT that many companies have not tackled is the sourcing of IT products and services where procurement policies are not uniform or controlled as well as they should be. Companies spend a great deal of time evaluating an initial large expenditure, but they pay little attention to smaller, ongoing expenses that can add up. Uniform sourcing and procurement policies can cut costs in all areas.

- **Contract management.** In IT, many contracts with service, software, and hardware providers are not managed or reviewed. Overpayments in maintenance, service-level agreements, usage, and other areas frequently occur. Reviewing and managing contracts can save significant revenues. Companies should review all maintenance contracts yearly to see if they should either downgrade service levels or discontinue paying maintenance. For older technologies that provide limited support, it is possible to renegotiate terms with the threat of cancellation.

- **Asset utilization.** It is easy to overbuy in an age where Intel-based servers pop up within a company like dandelions on a lawn. Companies should review the installed base and configurations of all hardware and storage and look for consolidation savings. This is often a quick and easy way to cut back on certain hardware and software costs. Labor costs may also be decreased.

Even the best companies have found areas that can be trimmed. A best practice in this area is a relentless ongoing search for cost savings.

Medium strength: the 20 to 40 percent solution

The next range of potential cuts is where most companies reside—somewhere between the Path of Profits and the Path of Problems. Such companies can look for significant cost reductions in all areas of spending. Cuts can range from the merely uncomfortable to the extremely painful, because certain staff will be replaced by less expensive offshore labor.

These companies have a wide range of effectiveness. They may be using technology quite well but at an artificially high cost. They will have the hardest time making cuts, because they believe they have been successful and do not need to reduce their IT budgets. These companies are often in industries that have been immune to budget pressures and cost concerns.

To deliver effective spending cuts, business groups need to be included in these exercises. Certain operational efficiencies led by IT groups have the potential to cut spending by more than 20 percent. In these instances, business groups should examine new IT investments and ongoing expenditures. These expenditures can be linked back to the business at hand. With this knowledge, such groups often discover technologies that are not used or are too expensive for the benefit derived. Higher visibility is the only way these higher levels of cuts can be accomplished.

Beyond simple, operational cuts made with an IT-only oriented approach, others must be considered:

- **Inclusive offshoring.** Many organizations can drastically slash external domestic consultants and cut specific internal labor by replacing them with offshore capabilities. Most areas of service and labor should be investigated, ranging from technical call centers, to tactical programming, to maintenance, to project implementation. Today, only a few skills cannot be transferred to offshore providers; these mostly consist of areas requiring close customer intimacy. "In the United States, the value is business knowledge, which is something that can never be transferred to India," said Chandrasekaran Natarajan, corporate vice president of Tata Consultancy Services.

- **Hardware management/utilization.** The myriad of hardware technologies and storage devices that were installed in organizations long ago are often underutilized. "It's not sexy, but it works," said Gary Bloom, CEO of Veritas. He was speaking of storage management, but computer hardware management falls into the same boat. Companies with large distributed installed bases of NT, Linux, and Unix systems have both tactical and strategic ways to cut costs. These systems are utilized much less than their proprietary mainframe counterparts. Employees can also be eliminated, because there will be fewer machines to manage. Another way to cut costs is through the new on-demand hardware licensing schemes set forth by IBM and others, where hardware is used (and charged for) only during peak periods of use. This option reduces the need to purchase extra equipment that is used only during the occasional demand bubble.

- **Software management/utilization.** Companies can reduce their software costs by understanding how much software they have and what is actually being used. The savings with software management is two-pronged: managing the cost or maintenance of software and managing how much of the software is used.

- **Extended technology lifecycles.** The advent of the Internet and the creation of web service–based interfaces has helped to extend the workable life of hardware and software. PC lifecycles can be extended well beyond three to four years. At the same time, out-of-date software can be used longer and at lower cost because of the increasingly prevalent use of web services and specifications such as XML, SOAP, and others.

Many technologists caution against such cuts, because they believe companies will become too enamored with the cost cleaver and cut spending past the bone. Such fears are justified, but they can be minimized when different metrics and approaches are used to cut back. For example, rather than tell an IT group that it needs to cut 20 percent of its staff, request a 15 percent decrease in labor and service expenses, or suggest delivering a certain level of service at a given cost. This approach allows technology managers to take a fresh look at how their labor is segmented and priced. Business and IT groups need to work together closely to see what works and what doesn't.

Extra strength: the 40 percent plus solution

Most companies that have the potential to cut more than 40 percent of their technology costs currently have large operational challenges. They have let spending get out of hand for many years. Such companies have a wide variety of technologies, software packages, and staff that grew quickly during the good times. They are not much different than the companies in the prior bracket, but they spend much more and get much less from their technology investments. The same opportunities for reductions exist for this group that exist for the others. The big difference is that the cuts will be much greater, as will the resistance to change.

To obtain this level of reduction, companies must have strong business and technology advocates who are looking not only at the levels of technology spending but also at the business benefits derived. Together, the technology and business groups can discover ways to efficiently wed technology to business benefits.

The three Cs of cost cutting

Cutting technology costs effectively requires both business and technology groups to examine the interplay between pure technology and how it is used. These two groups jointly drive the cost-reduction exercise: Technology examines hardware, software, and service agreements; and business examines utilization and payback of a deployed technology.

A three-step process, illustrated in the chart on the next page, should be considered. Each step addresses a different cost area: operational efficiency, asset/labor efficiency, and technology business efficiency. In other words, capacity, capital, and cleverness:

- **Capacity.** Operational efficiencies are a good place to start when looking for cost reductions. In general, they are not disruptive to companies because they focus on doing a better job with the resources a company already has. IT groups by themselves can focus on operational efficiencies. This effort focuses on determining a technology group's overall capacity, how it can be better utilized, and how to make the appropriate changes. With operational efficiencies, companies look to maximize current technology investments to get more speed, capacity, and use out of current equipment and labor.

- **Capital.** The next area of focus is asset/labor efficiency. Rather than explore how much of a given asset (or worker) is used, it examines how much is needed. This need is defined by both technologically oriented performance metrics (e.g., how many servers does my company really need?) and business metrics (e.g., how many licenses of a particular software product are needed/used?). This cost cutting occurs because technology and business groups agree on which technologies address business needs. Because both groups understand how much is being spent on technology, the business groups can understand the profile of technology spending and correlate it with use. This allows the technology and business groups to see where cuts can be made.

- **Cleverness.** The final area of focus is business efficiency. Technology business efficiency focuses on how clever companies are in their overall use of technology. Companies that attempt to do more with less and understand the benefit that technology delivers will be able to remove the last bit of excess from their IT systems. These groups question all IT investments and their relationship to corporate performance. This last

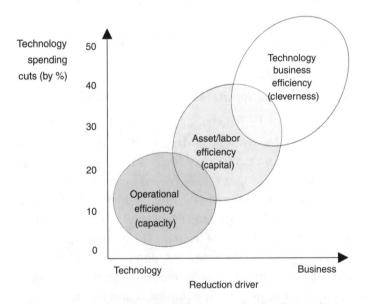

The three Cs of cost cutting. Both business and technology units must contribute to how IT costs can be reduced within a company. The bottom axis represents the group that dominates the cost-reduction exercise for a given phase. Technologists by themselves can drive cost reductions, but the highest efficiencies and spending cuts require technology and business groups to work together.

means of cost cutting is led by business groups that focus on investment return and whether a technology provides a benefit to the corporation. The evaluation metrics include factors such as gross margins, customer satisfaction, and increase in sales. The technology must have a direct correlation with a business value—if it does not, then it needs to be further evaluated and considered.

Putting the three Cs together

Taken together, these three steps are iterative and cycle back on each other as part of a continuous process, as the chart below shows. As each step is successfully completed, the next step should be attempted. If problems arise, then the company should cycle back to the prior step. The following example illustrates how companies can step through the three Cs.

Assume a company has made an investment in a sales-force automation (SFA) system, which has functions including forecasting,

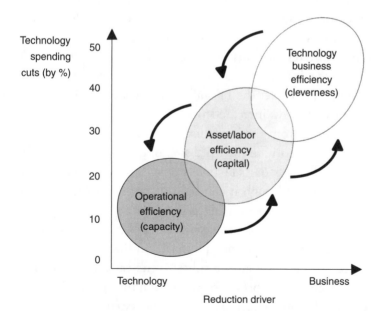

Iterative cost-cutting steps. The three steps to cutting costs are iterative and cycle back on each other. Upon the successful completion of a single step, the next step is attempted. However, if problems arise in the evaluation of a certain type of technology, then the prior step is reevaluated and reconsidered.

reporting and analysis, activity management, lead tracking, and customer management. The first-level evaluation is purely operational and looks at capacity: How many servers are used? Is the application performing at the required level? Are the correct licensing levels being supported? These areas of evaluation and potential improvement can be accomplished by the IT group. The evaluation of capacity looks only at how to get more from a current investment in order to lower costs in certain areas.

After capacity is analyzed, the next step is to evaluate how much capital is being invested in the application as well as the application's efficiency. For this analysis, business managers in the sales and/or operational groups should be brought in to examine all areas of spending for SFA and apply it to how a given technology is being used: How much is being spent to maintain the application? Are sales groups actually using the tool? Is there a perceived benefit from the cost of SFA? Are there less expensive ways to accomplish the same business goals?

In this step, the company begins to discover whether its capital investment in SFA is properly aligned with the business goals at hand. After analysis, one conclusion may be that only a few of the sales representatives use the system, but they use it well. This conclusion permits different actions to be considered. One action is that operational efficiencies can be realized by dropping/cutting licenses. Such a decision will also let the IT staff cycle back to the first phase of the exercise to review increased operational efficiencies for the application resulting from the lower user count.

This takes the company to the third step of determining the technology business efficiency of its IT investment. This is not just a simple ROI calculation (although it can be) but rather a focus on how well the technology is used to achieve business goals. This type of analysis is driven by business groups with support from technologists. In the case of SFA, the company may find that use of the currently installed package taps into a subset of its capabilities. It may also find that the initially expected benefits from the application have not occurred. In addition, because so few employees use the software, it may be ill suited to realizing the corporation's business goals.

These types of findings require the company to decide whether to better incorporate the technology into the sales cycle with an expected benefit to be derived or to discontinue or minimize its use. This decision then cycles back into the prior two loops for further cuts.

The final phase of analysis determines how clever the company has been in using technology. The issue it explores is not whether a technology is inherently good or bad, but rather whether its use (or misuse) generates a positive business return. The same technology implemented in different companies can have vastly different results. This is the highest level of analysis a company can engage in. For this analysis, business benchmarks are essential. So for the SFA investment, a correlation between higher customer close rates (percentage of prospective customers who buy), increased sales per customer, and shortened time for sales cycles are key metrics that should be examined.

As companies look to strip away costs and evaluate the cleverness of their technology purchases, each step brings technologists and business leaders closer together. This proximity creates a synergy that will help both groups discover what they need to do to improve their company. Unfortunately, companies have only recently begun to create such synergies to understand the relationships between corporate cost drivers and technology expenses. For companies to walk on the Path of Profits, they must better understand what technologies they have and how they use them.

Born to be cautious

As companies begin this series of evaluations, they need to determine their final destination. Unless organizations can make changes to accommodate the strategic use of technology, their best path may be the one that minimizes all spending. This is the path suggested (and in fact encouraged) by Nicholas Carr in his *Harvard Business Review* article. It is the right choice for companies that have at least a few of the following attributes and are unable to change them:

- **See IT as a commodity.** For companies and managers that take this view, cost cutting should be the only focus. Business gains from better use of technology will be tough to execute in such an environment. By minimizing the costs of technology, such companies also minimize the potential for failures and wasted expenditures.

- **Conservative with regard to change.** Effective use of technology beyond the Path of Pennies requires a bit of imagination and carefully managed risk-taking. Some projects will *not* derive a cost benefit. A willingness to experiment is essential. The best benefits for technology often cut across departmental and organizational boundaries, so companies that are unwilling to change or alter current practices can only use technology to automate well-defined manual processes that already exist. Those processes should be commonly known and automated by a technology package that can be easily bought and installed at a low cost.

- **Organizational walls between business and technology units.** Without ample sharing of communication and budget responsibilities between business and technology groups, there is little chance of realizing higher benefits and lower costs. These are the same walls that facilitate acrimony and misunderstanding between the groups. If these walls cannot be removed, then IT groups must act as a single contractor and keep costs low. Business groups should not look to technology as a way to improve corporate profitability or change costs.

- **No business data or benchmarks.** IT groups can only do so much in deploying technology. If they do not have proper guidelines or metrics by which a project can be viewed as a success or failure (or going in the right direction), a project that is a technological success can easily become a business failure. Business units need to provide benchmarks to guide both groups in evaluating their progress (and their investments) when a new technology is implemented.

- **Departmental mindsets.** Effective cost reductions and technology use require unequal sacrifices and layoffs from different groups. The benefits that one group enjoys from a technology project may require layoffs from a different group. In today's cost-driven environment, IT managers generally suffer the most from budget and staff cuts. Favorite business applications that don't generate a proper return are also generally challenged. Unless all groups are willing to accept such changes and share in the pain, projects that generate good business returns will be difficult to find and execute.

Companies that admit they cannot or will not change these factors are not business leaders, but followers. These companies have given up on bettering who they are regardless of how much or little technology they choose to use.

GETTING ON THE RIGHT PATH

Regardless of which IT spending path is chosen, the best path is the one where business and technology groups work together. This mixing is not easy, because these two cultures come from very different perspectives. Technology groups focus on how to better spread technology throughout a corporation. They are trained, educated, and compensated to get systems to work as specified. Business groups focus on executing various corporate strategies in areas such as marketing, logistics, sales, and operations. They are trained, educated, and compensated to exceed yearly business goals.

Problems with overspending (or underspending) can come from a misalignment of values, perceptions, and knowledge of how technology should be used in pursuit of a business strategy. English philosopher C.P. Snow pointed out in his book *The Two Cultures* that the cultures of the arts and sciences have been and continue to be split due to a lack of common education and values.[2] The same can be said of business groups and technologists within companies.

As a few companies have shown, however, when these two groups come together, a powerful synergy can be created that allows corporations to realize the best of both worlds: technological prowess combined with business execution. This new world of costs and benefits has become increasingly attractive to buyers of technology. As they execute this new strategy, their approach will dramatically change the way in which technology is sold. Technology suppliers (and employees) of the future must prepare themselves for the changes ahead if they want to maintain their industry positions and jobs.

CHAPTER ELEVEN

IT'S NOT
BUSINESS AS USUAL

*I am not waiting for the days when a customer needs 1,000
seats and buys 3,000. Those days are not coming back.*
—Sanjay Kumar, CEO,
Computer Associates

"WHY DO PEOPLE NEED A SALES FORCE?" complained
Hasso Plattner, then CEO (currently the supervi-
sory board chairman) of SAP. It was early spring
in 1998, and the *spargel* (white asparagus) were
pushing their heads through the dirt in the fields that surround
SAP's corporate headquarters in Waldorf, Germany. Plattner wasn't
really looking for an answer from me; he often posed such rhetori-
cal questions.

"If customers just looked things up on the Web and talked to
some of our people over the phone, they would figure out that we
had what they needed, and that would be that," he stated firmly.

"But Hasso, it's not that simple," I protested. "People need to be sold to. That is the nature of business. If you didn't have a sales force, you would be a much smaller company."

He looked at me quizzically and then shrugged his shoulders. "You are probably correct. But still it's a real waste of time and money." We went on to a different topic.

As Plattner implied, there is something wrong with the way large technology purchases are made. As companies reevaluate their technology buys, sellers must begin to reassess their business models and how they generate profits. New initiatives might include the following:

- **Cutting the expense base by 20 to 40 percent.** Many technology companies will never become profitable in the new spending environment unless they change the way they manage their business. This requires an operational focus and skill set that many companies today do not have.

- **Changing selling and support models.** Technology buyers have always assumed much of the risk for any given project. This risk will start to shift from buyers to sellers, requiring a change in selling, support, and finance models. The successful technology business model of the future will be oriented toward services and subscription revenue. The services sector will become a larger revenue component than it has been in the past. The rate of development and number of new products will decline.

- **Focusing on a small target market and/or planning to be acquired.** The vendor landscape of the future will be dotted with a few large (multibillion-dollar) companies and many small vendors with revenues no greater than $500 million, most under $100 million. Only those companies with a realistic and narrow focus will survive. The best of these will be acquired.

- **Emulating consumer technology sales and support models.** To decrease costs, vendors will need to standardize offerings, minimize expensive customization, and make their technology easy to use and install. Sellers of corporate IT should look to consumer technology companies for some pointers.

Sellers will not need to make all of these changes to their business models in order to succeed, but status quo operations will not continue to work much longer. First, companies must find ways to eliminate excess costs.

SELLING TECHNOLOGY IS EXPENSIVE

Selling technology to corporations often requires a large, highly compensated sales and marketing force that spends much of its time selling a wide variety of high-priced wares. Before a buyer makes a technology purchase, it stages complex and expensive "bake-offs" between competing vendors. At the end of this contest, one seller emerges victorious and often (but not always) signs a large contract, with a hefty initial lump-sum payment.

After a contract is signed, another set of complexities comes into play. While certain purchases can be easily installed, others require customization of software and services to meet the company's business needs. As new technologies are added, they must be integrated with complementary solutions. This requires expensive and time-consuming changes to many corporate systems.

These customer requirements create a need for consulting services, products, and product add-ons. The expensive and complex nature of corporate IT has created an equally expensive and complex set of vendor costs. This complexity is reflected in the expense models of software and service companies, as shown in the table below.

Technology company cost models. Over the last decade, hardware companies have had to dramatically change their business models because of the impact of commodity microprocessor technology. Software and service companies are being faced with the same cost challenges.

(As a % of revenues)	Software	Services	Hardware
Cost of revenue	5–20%	40–80%	60–85%
Gross margins	95–80%	60–20%	40–15%
R&D	5–25%	0–0.5%	3–15%
Sales/marketing	30–40%	5–20%	3–15%
Administration	5–20%	5–15%	5–15%
Pretax margins	Up to 40%	Up to 30%	Up to 20%
Leading example	Microsoft	Wipro (based in India)	Dell

Unlike services and hardware companies, software companies typically have a high gross profit margin—some as high as 95 percent. Because the cost of goods is low, the potential for profits is high. Oracle is one of many software vendors that has been able to increase its margins for years through simple operational efficiencies.[1] But in spite of this large markup, few software companies make a profit during their early years. These gross margins get whittled away by many factors, particularly R&D and sales and marketing costs. Once established with a good customer base, software companies can enjoy pretax margins of 15 to 25 percent; Microsoft's pretax margins are about 40 percent.

The profit potential at service companies is slightly less, as the cost of goods sold (e.g., salaries and bonuses to consultants) is much higher than for software (although the R&D and sales/marketing expenses are less). With rates as high as $300 per hour for high-end consultants and $1,000 per day or more for engineers, service companies can generate a great deal of revenue. Hardware companies, on the other hand, have seen over a decade of ruthless price cutting and market consolidation, and have trimmed costs (and prices) to the bone.

Making cuts

When buyers were willing to pay top dollar for technology, the business models of software and services were lucrative for both employees and stockholders. Employees were paid exceedingly well, and stockholders were able to make lots of money on the revenue run-ups. Today, customers are no longer willing to pay top dollar for software or services. If buyers are able to remove 20 to 40 percent of IT costs from their budgets, so must service and software providers. Software companies can make cuts in the following areas:

- **Sales and marketing (S&M).** Software companies spend upward of 40 percent of their total revenue in this area. "Companies need to be much more innovative in how they sell," according to Romesh Wadhwani, managing partner, Symphony Technology Group, a venture capital company. One of Symphony Technology's strategies is to purchase high-quality technology companies that are suffering from poor operational management. "More selling will need to be done by phone, over the Web, and not by large teams of experts that descend 15 to 20 times onto a potential customer's site," Wadhwani believes. By creating effective strategies, companies should be able to cut their S&M spending down to 25 percent or less of total revenue. Use of telephone sales, "webinars," and other methods will help companies keep costs down. Spending can drop even further if companies create a segmented and focused selling structure so that representatives have the opportunity to become more knowledgeable about individual customers' business needs. This requires the creation of separate sales teams, a structure similar to that found in consulting companies (which have teams of domain-rich experts).

- **Research and development (R&D).** R&D is ripe for offshoring. Many software vendors are exploring ways to set up their development abroad and hope to cut as much as 40 percent of their total R&D costs. This is not as difficult as it might sound. Many of a company's well-defined coding and development activities can be effectively outsourced for new applications and ongoing maintenance. Overall systems design, technical and business-process intellectual property, architecture, and definition of customer requirements and specific add-ons requiring close customer contact can remain in the home office.

- **General and administrative (G&A).** Many IT CEOs have little operational focus and overspend on technology, buildings, furniture, and benefits. If technology companies followed the example of some cost-focused industries such as oil and gas, total G&A expenses would consume less than 10 percent of total revenue. For example, SAP's G&A expense is about 6 percent of revenue. Simple belt tightening can reduce, or even eliminate, many costs.

- **Services.** Better management of consulting resources can chop 10 to 20 percent off total costs, but the largest impact will be from shifting certain labor to India and other nations. One mid-step move being taken by some companies is the redeployment of technologists in less-expensive, mid-America locations from more expensive East and West Coast ones.

Web-based service and support programs are also helping many companies improve their cost structures.

These moves will be tough for an industry not accustomed to belt tightening. "Out of one thousand companies, perhaps one to two hundred will be able to make it. But they will need inspired leaders... and unfortunately there is a dearth of great CEOs in the software industry," according to Wadhwani.

CHANGING THE RISK EQUATION

Cost cutting is only one of the changes that will be needed to meet the challenges of the future in the technology markets. As buyers become less willing to make large technology investments up front, sellers must sell incrementally and take on more of the risk themselves. A number of factors determine if the buyer will see a positive return on its investment. Regardless, under today's selling schemes,

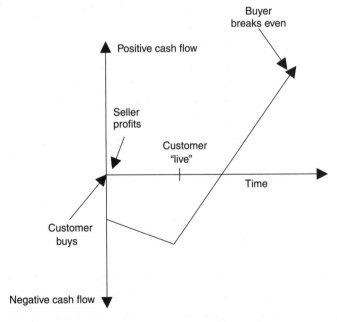

Cash flow from technology investments. With most technology purchases, the buyer assumes all the risk for technology implementations. Typically, the seller of software or hardware profits the instant a purchase order has been signed. The buyer, however, does not benefit until after a lengthy implementation cycle.

the seller always profits by being paid for the product and services delivered, as shown in the previous chart.

Sellers rationalize this schism by citing their risks: high up-front costs of a direct sales force and large marketing expenses. For every $500,000 deal a company wins, it may spend $200,000 in sales costs on deals it does *not* close. This money is spent on executive travel, sales meetings with prospects, the transportation of technical support and equipment to the prospect, and other expenses. This way of doing business has necessitated a high initial software charge in order to cover these expenses. As technology sellers have had to absorb the often high up-front costs of selling (often many times that of R&D), buyers have had to absorb high initial licensing fees.

One way that technology buyers and sellers can break this cycle is by flipping the risk equation, with sellers assuming more of the risk and getting paid according to how much a technology is used. At the same time, buyers must reconsider how much direct, on-site effort they should expect for free from sellers. In effect, sellers need to do a better job of understanding the business needs of a company, the potential for success, and what it takes to make the implementation successful. Rather than look for any customer with an open wallet, salespeople need to search out companies that are likely to implement a solution successfully. Sellers must deploy their sales forces carefully to close prospects. Buyers may have to start paying sellers for certain parts of an evaluation that they are used to getting for free. Change is required on both sides.

Today, many companies that purchase technology pay an up-front, onetime license fee, a custom consulting fee, and an ongoing maintenance and support fee. Once sellers start to assume the risk, customers will pay an initial setup fee, a yearly hookup fee (to have access to the technology), and possibly a usage fee. This is exactly the way utilities, such as telephone, power, and cable companies, charge for their services.

Under this type of sales model, customers will pay a low fee to the vendor until the system goes live. This fee should barely (at best) cover the vendor's installation cost of its technology. Future payment streams will vary based on usage and acceptance, but will flow to the technology vendor like an annuity. If the system doesn't work for some reason, the vendor won't get paid. The incentive for the vendor to sell such an offering is a sharing of returns; as a technology becomes more valuable and more widely deployed, a vendor will be paid more. Over a period of time, the vendor will receive more money from the buyer, and the buyer will be exposed to less risk with each technology decision than under the current model. Like the utility companies, sellers can lock in buyers because changing providers would be an expensive proposition (integration costs, training fees, and so forth).

This type of selling requires different expectations from the buyer and seller. The buyer should recognize that it is assuming a lower risk in exchange for a long-term relationship with the seller. The seller must have a financial model that permits it to deliver services and products well ahead of recognized revenues. It will require greater access to capital and a willingness to accept slower, albeit more consistent, revenue growth.

Sales alternatives

Two selling mechanisms can facilitate this type of model: subscription- and value-based licensing. *Subscription-based licensing* is a scheme in which the buyer pays only for what is used at any given point in time. Metrics used for billing include the number of employee or customer records, the number of customer calls, bandwidth used, or any other type of measurement that ties in to actual use.

Both large and small technology vendors have attempted this type of selling. For example, Descartes Systems Group, of Waterloo, Canada, a $70 million logistics vendor that sells solutions for optimizing transportation operations, has been selling technology subscriptions for the past four years.

"To do this as a public company was like sticking bamboo shoots up your fingernails," said Art Mesher, chief logistics officer. "We have been at this for four years, and 70 to 75 percent of all our revenues are recurring." As of mid-2003, Descartes was very close to breaking even. Descartes installs a starter kit at the site of every customer for a fixed fee; the customer is then billed for a monthly access fee and individual transaction fee. On paper, Descartes looks just like the telephone company.

For Descartes to be successful, it must ensure that its clients are happy with the service. If they don't use it, Descartes doesn't get paid. Simple. "This model brings back truth and consequences: If you don't tell the truth [about what you can do], you have massive consequences. You wind up doing a pilot and then you don't get paid, and that is brutal," explained Mesher.

Both IBM and Computer Associates (CA) are selling products using *on-demand pricing*, a variant of subscription-based pricing. On-demand pricing permits a buyer to pay only for the technology it uses at any given point in time, even when most of the technology is installed on site.

For instance, one of CA's airline customers pays for a certain software functionality based on passenger miles flown. CA's revenues from this customer go up and down depending on how successful the airline is in loading its planes with people, even though CA's software has little to do with this metric. The fees are tied to *business* metrics of the software's use rather than *technical* metrics, such as the range of computer hardware (high or low end) or the number of users.

In the summer of 2003, IBM signed an exclusive agreement with toymaker LEGO to provide it with all of its computer hardware systems, replacing those of competitor Hewlett-Packard.[2] The deal hinged on the agreement that LEGO pay IBM only for the computing power it uses. LEGO won't have to purchase extra systems to ensure that its IT works well during the peak Christmas season. Instead, it will be able to use IBM hardware on demand. LEGO expects its computing costs to be reduced by at least 30 percent.

The subscription model also changes the dynamics of buying. The last-ditch sales force heroics that have become all too familiar to technology buyers are replaced with a continuous, predictable, revenue stream. Revenues become smoother with the disappearance of last-minute surprises.

But the transformation can also result in large revenue drops for companies that have depended on license sales. CA's revenues for its fiscal year 2000 were $6.1 billion, with a $1 billion profit. Moving to on-demand pricing, along with other factors, reset revenue measurements and led to fiscal year 2003 revenues of $3.1 billion and a loss of $260 million. IBM, on the other hand, generates more than half of its revenue from services and is not as exposed to this pricing shock as other vendors.

The other pricing mechanism is value based. With *value-based pricing*, the provider is paid only when certain value metrics are met. Such metrics include reduced inventory levels, a climb in the number of customers, and a decline in telephone calls that a person must handle. This type of pricing puts buyer and seller at risk since payments can vary widely; this approach has had limited success.

The key to getting either of these selling alternatives to work is an understanding of the value of various technologies, as well as the cost and revenue models under which they operate. Both techniques require sellers to obtain revenue at a slow initial rate, and both result in reduced initial software license revenues. As companies face these declining license sales, they have but one way to increase their revenues dramatically: services.

Selling services

I recall a conversation with Larry Ellison, CEO of Oracle, that took place in the late 1990s. We were discussing how Oracle would grow in the future. "So when will you have more revenues from services than from software licenses?" I casually asked.

"What are you talking about? That will never happen!" he shot back, agitated. "That's not part of our corporate strategy."

"I know that is not part of your strategy, but it appears to be happening anyway," I pointed out. "What is so wrong with services?"

I thought there was potential for increased revenue in services—Ellison did not.

And he wasn't the only one. This lack of desire to extend service offerings reflected how certain technology vendors, mostly software vendors, did not want a large role in solving some of the deeper business problems of their clients. More services for software companies often meant lower gross margins and thus lower stock prices. In effect, Wall Street told software vendors to stay away from services. But that was a mistake for both buyers and sellers.

Most buyers never realize all of the benefits that can be derived from a given technology and use only a fraction of the total capability of the systems they purchase. A technology provider should therefore focus on teaching the customer best practices that will allow it to make better use of the technology it has purchased to ensure the maximum business benefit. The provider can also demonstrate ways to exploit portions of the solution the customer has not yet enabled and deliver a highly valued service. Everyone wins. It is no surprise that IBM is among the most aggressive of providers looking to expand their services offerings.

Here are some opportunities for expanding services:

- **Lifecycle management.** This entails upgrading and maintaining the infrastructure of a given technology. Companies spend a great deal of money maintaining a rapidly changing array of technologies.

- **Integration and modification.** This involves integrating and modifying existing systems to coexist with new technology purchases. Business unit changes and new technology purchases will continue to create a need for such services.

- **Asset management.** Every year, you should measure how an application is being used to ensure that no money is being left on the table.

- **Operational efficiencies.** IT is one of the last disciplines to focus on lowering costs while delivering the same level of service. Operational efficiencies can be drawn from nearly all IT facilities and represent a good market opportunity.

- **Outsourcing.** Besides selling software or services, technology companies have an opportunity to increase their revenue by offering outsourcing contracts to customers. Such offerings can range from technical infrastructure all the way to business processes.

Benchmarking is one of many new service offerings that could emerge. Benchmarking can be twofold; the simplest benchmark is to compare how many resources are used to operate any given system versus another. Results can be used to tweak operational efficiencies. The next benchmark indicates how well a company uses a given technology and how its operation affects corporate results.

For this type of service offering, a company will need to have three groups of experts:

- Technologists, who know the capabilities of the software
- Industry experts who are familiar with the business drivers for any given vertical industry
- Functional experts, who bring best practices for various application types to customers

The tendency to see every problem as a nail to be pounded by a technology hammer must be replaced by a subtler view, one that ultimately provides more value to the buyer.

This strategy of enhanced service was executed successfully by PeopleSoft through much of the 1990s. PeopleSoft assigned a variety of customer service experts to its clients after a product was sold. These experts ensured that clients were satisfied with their software and understood all of its capabilities. This approach is one of the reasons PeopleSoft ranks among the leading software vendors in customer satisfaction.

SMALLER MARKETS, SMALLER TARGETS

The current spending squeeze will accelerate the market consolidation trend. In the early 1990s, a large software vendor such as Cullinet Software or Dun & Bradstreet had annual revenues in the range of $300 million to $500 million. Today, that range starts at $3 billion. The broadening reach of multibillion-dollar vendors, combined with the desire of buyers to limit their purchases to a smaller number of sellers, makes it difficult for a small, generic, or unfocused company to succeed.

As a result of this trend, we can divide sellers into two groups, as you can see in the chart on the next page. The first is composed of a few large companies that offer a broad suite of products (which, as a group, provide a medium depth of functionality). Such companies include Computer Associates, IBM, Microsoft, Oracle, and SAP. Their yearly revenue is in the billions of dollars. Certain products in the group may have advanced functionality and capabilities, particularly in areas central to the companies' initial success. For example,

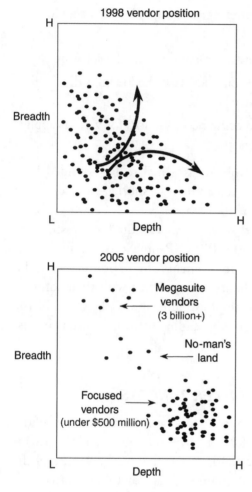

Software vendor positioning by breadth versus depth of offerings. The software market is quickly evolving into a two-tiered system where successful vendors will either be very large and have a broad suite of offerings or very focused and relatively small. Companies that attempt to bridge both worlds will have only a slight chance of success.[3]

SAP's financial software is considered strong, while its operational software for the retail sector has limited capabilities.

The second group consists of small vendors that have focused on a specific piece of business functionality and/or a vertical market. Their yearly revenue is less than $500 million—in many cases less than $100 million. Companies in this category include Aspen Technology, a manufacturing software company; Ariba, a procurement vendor; and retail vendor QRS Corp. These vendors are able to succeed because they solve a specific problem well. Their target market is limited, which for the most part keeps them out of the competitive spotlight of the largest software vendors.

The worst place for a technology vendor to be is somewhere between these extremes. This makes them more attractive for acquisition by large players, and their products typically lack the depth of the solutions sold by smaller competitors. The acquisition of JD Edwards by PeopleSoft in the summer of 2003 is a good example of a company that was caught in the middle.

> **Note**
> The steps needed for success in high-technology markets have been well documented by Geoffrey A. Moore in his book *Crossing the Chasm* (HarperBusiness, 2002).

With a tougher market ahead, software companies must choose between breadth of function and focus of market (domain expertise). Historically, many vendors have approached market segmentation by letting their sales force define their markets for them, rather than making a conscious effort to define a potential client base. Such companies must change their approach to be successful in the future.

SHRINK-WRAPPING ENTERPRISE SOFTWARE?

Common wisdom dictates that enterprise software be expensive and complex. This wisdom represents the very reasons why many large IT systems have failed in the past. Technological complexity will always exist, but the most successful vendors of the future will be the ones that can minimize a user's exposure to this complexity. Sellers of corporate IT must adopt certain characteristics of companies that focus on *consumer* sales.

"When are you going to shrink-wrap this software?" Lee Wylie asked another unsuspecting software vendor in the early 1990s. Lee, my first boss at Gartner, believed that one of the most important criteria for systems was ease of use and installation. Lee had previously run an Apple Computer dealership, had been an executive at IBM, and had helped design all the plant-floor systems for the innovative General Motors Saturn plant in Tennessee.

In 1991, it was inconceivable to sell complex software that could simply be loaded into a computer and run. But Lee kept banging away at this point, saying that this was what people needed to do to be successful in the market.

Lee's words of wisdom came to mind recently when a company commissioned me to survey its client base. The company wanted to know what its customers perceived as the real value of its application suite. Going into the survey, the company and I both assumed that the answer would be some combination of (a) technology platform and (b) functional superiority. We couldn't have been more wrong.

"Ease of use, ease of use, ease of use," said one interviewee.

"Simple to use and a low-cost implementation," said another.

"No training, and the package is very accessible," said a third.

My client and I were both surprised at these results.

Companies now expect something different from their enterprise technology suppliers. To adopt a consumer technology delivery model, sellers must discard all of their traditional assumptions. Rather than attempt to sell a complex, highly customized system, sellers must move more toward a shrink-wrap model of product and service delivery. The solutions should be easy to use as well as simple to implement.

The table on the next page implies that significant changes will have to occur if these two distinct worlds are to merge. First, the corporate seller will need to bundle more of the value or services in the initial purchase price. This change implies a different mix of products as well as another reason to move to subscription-based pricing. Next, self-service or remote support should replace on-site support for the most part. Web-based applications as well as remote-device technologies (such as Symantec's pcAnywhere, a remote terminal program) are permitting some sellers to deploy this type of service at a low cost.

Look at the next set of comparisons in the table (sales/marketing ratios, user training, customization, and system integration). As you can see, corporate IT buying should strive for out-of-the-box, plug-it-in-and-get-it-working offerings. Customers will decide what they need, and they want the purchasing process to be as painless as possible. When combined with a subscription-based sales model, this simplicity can create powerful new competitors.

Comparison of consumer and corporate technology spending. Consumer and corporate technology spending/support patterns could not be more dissimilar than they are today. Ironically, some of the most successful companies selling to corporations are taking a page from the books of those that are successful in consumer sales.

	Consumer technology spending	Corporate technology spending
Initial purchase price/total lifecycle spending (does not consider subscription-based revenue)	80–90% (not including accessories, software)	10–20%
Support	Self-service, limited	On-site, extensive
Direct sales/marketing ratio	10/90%	70/30%
User training	Low	High
Customization	Low	High
Integration with other systems	Low	High

This is the position of Salesforce.com, which sells an online CRM solution to corporations. Formed in 1999, it has more than 7,300 customers and over 100,000 users, and as of this writing is expected to reach nearly $100 million in annual revenues by the end of 2003. Salesforce.com uses a subscription-based sales model, and its products are priced between $65 and $120 per month per user. In December 2003, it filed for an initial public offering (IPO).

"We are like Dell in that the focus is on a new distribution model," according to Jim Steele, president of worldwide operations. "We came out with a more cost-effective way to distribute [software]." Key to that distribution are the Internet and a service that's paid for as customers use it, at a cost that is lower than traditional enterprise software offerings.

A minimal amount of training, most of which is delivered over the Internet, is needed to become proficient with Salesforce.com's products. A small amount of customization and data transfer is required initially to get a customer online with Salesforce.com. To obtain the company's product, a customer need only access the Salesforce.com web site. Salesforce.com takes care of all the rest. Its price point and delivery scheme have forced the company to adopt a thrifty cost model.

"We knew that we would be charging an order of magnitude less than other companies, so from day one we had to run a very lean company," explained Steele. Salesforce.com uses only two Sun Solaris computers running an Oracle database to service all of its customers.

One of the major advantages that Salesforce.com has over traditional competitors is that it supports only a single version of its software on a single technology platform. This permits the company to better leverage its R&D investment; it does not have to spend time and money supporting a wide variety of technologies and software versions. Upgrades and changes are simple for the customer base because all companies work from a single system. This standardization minimizes customer downtime, confusion, and excessive expense. The company has enjoyed a positive cash flow since November 2001 and has been profitable since the spring of 2003.

Steele believes that companies are growing comfortable with the concept of online software or services for certain types of business processes: "ADP [Automatic Data Processing Inc.] has been doing this forever [for payroll] and no one has ever questioned the security of its offering. We follow that model."

Competitors may believe that the approach taken by Salesforce.com is viable only for small companies and those with uncomplicated sales operations. Keep in mind, though, that over a decade ago people said the same thing about PCs and Microsoft. For some companies, it may be better to get by with less than to fail with more.

MAKING THE CHANGE

Given all these factors, is there any chance that sellers will be able to extract more revenue from buyers than before? The short answer: no. Buyers will spend more on IT only if sellers are able to shoulder more of the initial risk (and expense) of implementing new systems. Sellers must be willing to back up their marketing rhetoric and claims with a low-risk, low-cost entry for buyers.

This change will not be easy for sellers. For example, moving over from a license-based to a subscription-based model is painful, and without considerable capital, even impossible. Descartes was able to do it because it had a great deal of cash relative to its revenues. "It took us $70 million in cash to get through all of this," said Mesher, describing Descartes's journey from a $40 million company based on license sales to a $70 million one based on subscriptions. Salesforce.com, however, had the advantage of being able to launch its company with lots of cash to offset initial losses and negative cash flow. In addition, the company started with a subscription-based revenue model, on which it based its operational spending.

For companies without cash or an initial subscription-based plan, it will be even harder, perhaps impossible, to make such a change. Altering current behaviors and making large spending cuts will put many employees out of work. Although some companies will evolve to new business models, evolution will be painful and unforgiving for most.

User acceptance is an additional challenge. As I explained earlier, companies have been cool to the concept of services and subscriptions, citing issues of security and a lack of customization, control, and integration with other existing corporate systems. In addition, there is a general lack of understanding among buyers regarding these methods of buying IT. A recent study on utility computing by Saugatuck Technology Inc. found that there is a fairly large gap between buyer and seller expectations of utility, or on-demand, computing.[4] This gap implies that buyers will not embrace such approaches quickly.

Buyers and sellers must meet somewhere in the middle. The number of sellers that can afford to lavish attention and money on a prospect that may not make a purchase is shrinking. Buyers wanting to pay less for technology need to become accustomed to new delivery and selling models. The old models just won't work anymore.

SURVIVAL GUIDE
FOR IT TECHS

All of the changes I've described will have a dramatic impact on U.S. technology employment. Savvy technologists should begin searching for safe job harbors. Job areas that will be less threatened than others include the following:

- **Government.** Although some government IT contracts are already being sent overseas, the growing cry to protect American jobs and potential legislation will likely minimize offshoring. With federal government IT spending growing at a healthy rate, this sector could be a good place for IT employees to look to continue their careers, though without the potential entrepreneurial upside to which some have become accustomed.

- **Vertical industries such as pharmaceutical, financial services.** If you understand how technology can solve thorny issues in a given industry, you will find your skills highly valued by both buyers and sellers. An understanding of paybacks and ROI is essential, as are skills that permit the wide dissemination of technology within an organization. Also important is the ability to think out of the box and understand where technology can have the greatest impact on business goals.

- **Project/program management.** As companies begin outsourcing or hiring employees in offshore firms, they will need people to manage projects that will be carried out in diverse locations. The ability to oversee multiple types of projects will make you attractive to these employers. Professionals will still be in demand to run and manage contracts, personnel, and a wide variety of providers.

- **Specialists.** There will always be a need for highly skilled specialists in hot and/or difficult technology areas, such as large enterprise applications, integration, and systems management. For a few, it's a good idea to maintain a skill set for older languages such as COBOL, FORTRAN, and, eventually, yesterday's darling, C++, as well as older mainframe technologies.

- **Highly focused, regional vendors/consultants.** Regional sellers and consultants that sell to small to medium-sized businesses (less than $250 million in annual revenue) will continue to fly under the radar screen of large vendors and offshore consultants. Such companies sell to local groceries, doctors, governments, and manufacturers. Their tight focus on expenses and delivery of value to local customers makes them less susceptible to industry-wide changes.

- **Customer fulfillment/support.** There will always be a need for on-site support personnel working directly with the customer or client for certain types of applications and tasks (self-service, remote, and online help not withstanding). This type of knowledge is increasingly important as companies seek to better understand customer needs. Efficient fulfillment/support helps increase customer satisfaction and therefore makes you more valuable to your employer.

- **Revenue generation.** The object of the game is always to get as close to the money as you can. Jobs that are physically attached to revenue represent lower risk than others (unless they are purely commodity functions). Certain end-user organizations may be able to take internally developed services and software and sell to the rest of the market, but it's a tough slog and fails more often than it succeeds.

- **Operations.** Although it may not be the most popular job in town, especially with the IT worker, the ability to suggest the "right" budget cuts will gain kudos from higher-management circles. In fact, operations management may be the key position in IT for years to come; eventually,

SURVIVAL GUIDE
FOR IT TECHS

someone is going to have to manage IT costs. This new breed could be groomed from pure operations experts or from veterans in the IT business.

Note
Today, baby-boomers make up half of the total U.S. workforce, according to the U.S. Department of Labor. Some economists believe that we can expect a job boom for highly skilled workers because of the likely retirement of baby-boomers over the next two decades. Nevertheless, companies will be pressured to move jobs offshore as well as automate them. In fact, a labor shortage could accelerate the move to offshore labor as a way to minimize the risk of being understaffed.

SURVIVAL GUIDE
FOR SELLERS

INCREASING SALES

To increase sales in these highly competitive times, vendors must offer substantial value and ensure that their customers know how to best take advantage of their technology. In order to increase revenues, sellers must understand the following:

- **Cost and revenue models vary by industry.** All industries have different metrics by which they are measured. In the airline industry, load factors and cost per passenger mile determine success; in retail, sales per square foot and same-store sales make all the difference. To increase sales, offer solutions designed to help companies improve such metrics, and price your products accordingly.

- **Introduce incremental value measurements, product offerings.** Prove that you can help your customers learn to walk before they run with your technology. Deliver a limited program in which you can easily demonstrate the potential of your technology. Benchmarks and short-term deliverables can be tied to payment schedules and an increase in buyer investment.

- **Match the business needs of customers to the technology.** If you hope to increase revenues in a tough spending environment, you must match products and services to your customers' business needs. The idea that every company has to optimize its inventory control or customer satisfaction capabilities is misleading. Technology spending should be tied to the business process that is *most* in need of improvement. Ensure that your products provide benefits that complement the strategic goals of your buyers.

- **Ensure the success of technology initiatives.** Although it may sound trite, sellers and buyers need to better align their interests to ensure success. Too many sellers have viewed their customers as a good learning experience rather than a partner or someone who could learn from

SURVIVAL GUIDE
FOR SELLERS

them. Take a more consultative view to ensure that your customer derives value from your technology. Make sure that the buyer has the appropriate environment to properly exploit your products or services. Without such support, most projects will fail to deliver a positive return.

SURVIVAL GUIDE
FOR START-UPS

FOUR-STEP PROCESS

Start-ups will have a tougher time in the future, and a different means of going to market and running a business will be required. Symphony Technology's Wadhwani has a simple, four-step process for start-up success:

- **Find a bold company willing to fund your idea.** The traditional returns that venture capitalists expect will not occur in the future, so a patient partner will be needed who is willing to make much less money over the long haul. Few venture capital companies are ready to admit that the boom days are over, so you will need a broad combination of backers, each contributing a smaller amount of money than in the past.

- **Create a focused R&D effort offshore.** The days of paying $100,000 or more to developers in expensive offices are over. In the future, most software development will take place in India and other nations. Keep a few key architects and product designers in the home office, but outsource everything else to low-cost, high-quality foreign offices. Someone who can manage such a divided effort successfully will be as important as the CTO of your company.

- **Sell and deliver based on a services model.** Although selling licenses may be an occasional necessary evil (because certain opportunities will present themselves), deliver your solution through a services/subscription model. Give it high priority, and tweak it to deliver positive cash flow. This means that your sales force must accurately identify prospects that are not only willing to make an initial deal but also likely to get it executed within their company so that follow-on business will occur. Key to success will be choosing which clients to pursue and which ones to ignore. A different type of

SURVIVAL GUIDE
FOR START-UPS

salesperson will be needed who not only can close a deal but also understands how technology can be implemented successfully at a client's site.

- **Use positive cash flows to fuel company growth.** Executed correctly, a service-based model should be able to deliver enough cash flow at $20 million in annual revenue so that a company can be self-sufficient. This requires a high degree of operational discipline as well as knowing which customers to pass up because they are unlikely to become profitable clients for you. Growth will not be as fast as in the past, but profitability will come more quickly to companies that follow this model.

STEPPING BACK
TO GET AHEAD

It would be a gross mistake to seek wholly within the field of technics for an answer to all the problems that have been raised by technics.

—Lewis Mumford, 20th-century historian[1]

The future ain't what it used to be.

—Baseball great Yogi Berra

A FTER THREE YEARS of lackluster performance, technology companies are waiting to hear that good times are just around the corner. For some, increased capital spending in the third quarter of 2003 was a good indication that a turnaround was imminent. But when Intel CEO Craig Barrett made a statement in the summer (and repeated it in the fall) that it was "too early to suggest it is a *total* turnaround,"[2] I knew things were not looking up after all.

Maybe companies will decide to return to their extravagant spending habits of the past—but more than likely, they won't. Consider the following:

- The next 15 years of IT spending will be led by business managers looking for results rather than an installed base of cool technology. New IT investments will be made with quantifiable goals rather than leaps of faith.

- IT-led productivity gains will occur only after companies get rid of excessive IT assets and programs. The most successful companies will be in cleanup mode for the next few years.

- The new business reality for sellers will continue to leave buyers in the driver's seat for years to come.

- The IT department of the future will have to manage distributed operations in many countries as well as understand how to apply IT strategically to business problems.

Smart buyers know that the time for change is now—and that they may need to take a step back in order to get ahead.

STEPPING BACK

The economic malaise of the early 21st century has meant that the pump stimulating IT spending has stopped...well, pumping. Before that pump is primed again—if it ever is—buyers must consider their options. Savvy folks are finding good role models in firms such as Harrah's, JetBlue, Motorola, and Merrill Lynch. These companies have succeeded at either keeping down or dramatically slashing IT expenses while maintaining positive business returns.

As these companies show, the use of new and exotic technologies is not needed. In fact, this book argues otherwise. While programming techniques and tools continue to provide fast and easy development of software, they alone will not alter the economic and management changes of technology deployment.

This is not to say that technological innovation will stop; it will, however, take a different direction than in the past. Many of the companies profiled in this book use technology innovatively, although they may not always use innovative technology. This implies that the IT buyers of the future will embark on a balancing act by using what they have innovatively and matching new technology buys against old technology cuts. Although budgets will remain stable or track slightly downward, large shifts within budgets will occur and will change the way monies are spent. Status quo budgeting will be under fire.

New technologies and approaches, such as radio-frequency identification, wireless, and Voice Over Internet Protocol (VOIP),[3] will be adopted, sometimes aggressively, but not without displacing other IT or business unit costs. Companies may continue to increase their IT spending with the hope of getting a bigger bang for their technology buck. Only the *disciplined* ones will successfully achieve their goals.

Some may say that these unconventional predictions are Malthusian—and that Thomas Malthus cried wolf and was wrong. This is true. However, his warning—that an exponential population explosion could not be sustained by crop yields that could expand at best arithmetically—was completely logical and sound. He could not have foreseen the breakthroughs in the course of history that would prevent his predicted global famines.

Actually, Malthus's writings probably inspired a few scientists to find solutions to the problems he squarely addressed, thereby "proving him wrong." So, let me say that if you can devise a way to get all companies to spend more on technology while deriving greater business benefits, please come forward. I will be the first to say "Thank you for proving me wrong!"

In the past, all revolutions in IT were led by a *new technology thing*. So unless there is, as Steve Jobs, Bill Gates, and others hint, a new technological gold mine that will revolutionize the way we do business, this next revolution will be led by a *new technology attitude*. That attitude is: spend less to get more.

The new stars

This change is not good news for corporate IT sellers or the stockholders who have become accustomed to rapid growth and high profits across the technology board. As the potential for corporate-related (versus consumer) technology growth comes under the microscope, it will become clear that the overall industry growth of the past will not be realized again.

Instead, small organizations in niche markets will become the stars of tomorrow. Companies with promising starts and radically different value propositions looking to take a different approach to complex problems—firms like VMware, BDNA, and Salesforce.com—have lean business models and approaches that will enable them to prosper. Established companies will have a harder time. (As this book was going to press, both VMware and Salesforce.com were realizing their stardom through a buyout and an IPO filing, respectively.)

IT sellers will have to modify their cost models to accommodate the new corporate appetite. Revenue pressure will be felt on all sides:

- Price increases will be difficult. The discounts of the past three years minimize the likelihood that buying technology will ever return to the "good old days."

- Service and consulting prices and margins will be pushed down by offshoring.

- Open source, freeware, Microsoft, and low-cost competitors will force price margins down.

- Hardware consumption will continue to slow due to better asset management and utilization.

Large, established vendors such as Accenture, IBM, Oracle, and SAP will need to learn how to grow their revenues and cut their expenses while experiencing significant margin deterioration with every passing year. Success is a moving target that will be hard to hit, even for those companies that are able to market to their installed base of customers.

TAKING THE PLEDGE: HOW TO MOVE AHEAD

While this situation sounds dire, it need not be. Both sellers and buyers can benefit, but only if they both pledge to replace business as usual with a dynamic model that promotes quality in IT. Perhaps the IT industry needs to take a page from the U.S. automobile industry in the mid-1980s, when Japanese automakers started to

Defects per 100 vehicles. The loss of market share to Japanese competitors was a key reason that U.S. automakers have focused on increasing quality over the last 15 years. IT buyers and sellers need to take a lesson from the auto industry. *Source: JD Power and Associates.*

Company	Defects per 100 vehicles in 1987	Defects per 100 vehicles in 2002
General Motors	180	127
Toyota	130	107

erode U.S. market share by introducing higher-quality (and less expensive) vehicles to the American public.

To address the difference in product quality and declining sales, U.S. automakers had to change everything they were used to doing. Today, American-made automobiles are better (as the table above shows) and cheaper than in the past. The same can be said for PCs and most other technology hardware, and this needs to happen for the rest of IT. Every year, companies should increase the quality of their IT by wringing more business benefits out of every technology dollar.

Software and service providers can tap into the same techniques used by automakers and PC manufacturers:

- **Production/deployment innovation.** The deployment of IT should combine business units providing the design and IT groups delivering the manufacture of the end products. When these groups work together, they can deliver a higher-quality product at a lower price. Providers can define technological innovation by executing a business process faster and less expensively, using different technology tools. The business process remains unchanged. Business innovation, on the other hand, will be derived from an altered business process that delivers increased efficiency or profit to a corporation. A technology deployment may facilitate this change in process.

- **Supplier cost reduction.** The core concept of productivity is based on delivering more value every year at a constant price. To meet this challenge, software and service firms can take advantage of new management techniques, diversified labor pools, and innovative technologies.

- **Job/product redistribution.** Companies must recognize what they can manufacture themselves cost-effectively and what they should buy from other suppliers. They need to find efficient ways to build products and deliver services to meet the new cost challenges. The ability to deploy design and production teams connected via the Internet makes this goal easier to achieve than with traditional operations.

None of these adjustments will be easy for buyers and sellers. In the years ahead, the IT survivors will be those companies and individuals who accept the fact that the business methods of the past were flawed.

Paradise regained?

When companies implement the sorts of changes I've described in this chapter, the rewards will be great for both buyers and sellers. Just as today's automobiles are an improvement over those of the 1980s, IT organizations and sellers will be better off a decade from

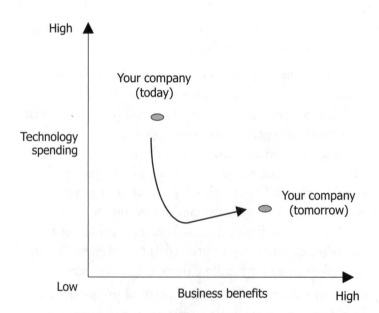

Getting on the Path of Profits. Companies should take some lessons from the auto and PC industries to increase their IT productivity. A combination of production innovation, supplier cost reduction, and job redistribution will be key for companies that hope to make the jump to the Path of Profits.

now. To move forward, most companies will have to take a few technology spending steps back, as illustrated in the chart on the previous page.

To realize this future, buyers and sellers must do the following:

- **Choose a path and go for it.** Technology can be either an albatross or an asset. The high ground in the market always goes to the swift. Sellers should determine the most optimal business model for their future and pursue it aggressively—even if it means years of losses and financial pain. Long-term survival is more important than short-term earnings.

- **Be realistic with choices.** The need to follow one path or the other is industry dependent. Be wary of following knee-jerk reactions and analysis. Sellers should be realistic in determining whether they can get to the needed financial model based on cash on hand and the potential to raise more capital. Selling a company from a position of strength rather than weakness is always better.

- **Don't attempt shortcuts.** Trying to get too much done too fast often leads to misguided goals and project obstacles. Companies will be pressured to cut technology costs while making substantial business changes. Create realistic timetables so you enjoy successful milestones.

- **Feel the pain.** Spread sacrifice and changes throughout the organization to facilitate buy-in. Rather than piling on spending and job cuts in a single area, look for synergistic changes throughout the corporation. But don't be afraid to take out the cleaver when necessary. Small, incremental cuts may hurt your company in the long run.

- **Execute, execute, execute.** Ensure that a leader with excellent operational capabilities is put in charge, and continue to benchmark progress and maintain a focus on realizing projects and goals.

Technology paradise lost will give way to paradise regained as companies execute these strategies. They will begin to discover that there is a relationship between *effective* IT spending and business benefits.

A BRIGHTER FUTURE

Are enough companies prepared to end the experimental era of IT? Are enough companies poised to embrace IT skillfully? I believe they are, but first they must tame the unruly beasts that live within their organization: the monsters of unresolved IT problems. For companies that can skillfully manage IT, the benefits will be substantial.

I have been watching IT for more than 25 years and have been disappointed with the unrealized potential. The IT world has a few masters but many more apprentices. The time is now for the apprentices to become masters in their own right and capitalize on the previous decades of experimentation. Corporations are ready to take the next step.

I am looking forward to the next 25 years as the time when IT management comes into its own as a practice to be honed, mastered, and profited from.

notes

CHAPTER 1

1 National Snow and Ice Data Center, "Larsen B Ice Shelf Collapses in Antarctica," March 2002; http://nsidc.org/iceshelves/ larsenb2002/.

2 *Moore's Law* refers to a conjecture made by Gordon Moore, one of Intel's founders. In 1965, Moore wrote a paper concerning the growth of semiconductor technology: "Cramming More Components onto Integrated Circuits," *Electronics* 38, no. 8 (April 1965); ftp://download.intel.com/research/silicon/moorespaper.pdf. His basic premise was that the number of transistors on an integrated circuit would double every few years. The conjecture was somewhat extended later, adding that the expansion would be at a constant price—that is, doubling of performance with no increase in price.

3 SAP is a leading software company based in Germany. It sells a wide variety of packaged applications in the areas of financial reporting, customer service, operations management, and others. It had revenues of 7.4 billion euros in 2002. The application of general-ledger functionality is part of an overall financial package including accounts payables, accounts receivable, financial controlling, asset management, and so on.

4 Morgan Stanley CIO Survey Series, Release 3.8 (December 2002). Every year, Morgan Stanley conducts a survey of more than 200 CIOs to determine IT buyer behavior and direction.

5   "The Truth About Tech," *CFO*, October 2002; http://
    www.cfo.com/article/1,5309,7887||M|406,00.html.

6   This is a composite number that is representative of what a wide
    variety of research companies including Gartner, META Group,
    and Forrester believe is spent on an existing installed base rather
    than on new technology initiatives. Individual estimates range from
    60 to 85 percent.

7   AMR Research, "Country Lifecycle Management," by Bruce Rich-
    ardson, April 2003. Executives at AMR, an IT market research firm
    based in Boston, MA, recently interviewed Mike Lawrie, senior vice
    president and group executive for IBM Global Sales and Distribu-
    tion, who indicated that IBM's long-term view of growth was dou-
    ble that of GDP growth.

CHAPTER 2

1   René Moreau, *The Computer Comes of Age: The People, the Hard-
    ware, and the Software*, trans. J. Howlett (Cambridge, MA: MIT
    Press, 1984), 48.

2   U.S. Department of Commerce, Bureau of Economic Analysis,
    "Private Fixed Investment by Type," National Income and Product
    Accounts Table 5.3.5; http://www.bea.gov/bea/dn/nipaweb/
    SelectTable.asp?Selected=N.

3   Ibid.

4   Ibid.

5   *Information processing equipment and software* includes office, com-
    puting, and accounting machinery; computers and peripheral
    equipment; communications equipment; photocopy instruments;
    and related equipment. *Equipment and software* includes informa-
    tion processing equipment and machinery and transportation
    equipment. *Corporate fixed investment* represents the total amount
    of all assets capitalized.

6   *Client-server technology* is an approach that takes the user interface
    (how the computer program appears to a user), data, and
    application processing (business rules and processes) and divides
    their use and locations between the machine a user has (a client)
    and another machine that is shared (a server). Internet-oriented
    architectures can be expressed by one extreme of client-server archi-
    tecture, the *thin client*, whereby nearly every aspect of processing,
    data, and user interface is handled on a server. Ironically, main-
    frame architectures first deployed in the 1960s use a thin-client
    implementation of computing.

7   *Standard cost* is an accounting procedure that assigns an average or preset cost to different processes and materials; *activity-based costing* takes a much more detailed view and assigns actual cost by product or product line by accounting for variations in labor, materials, and so on. For instance, over the course of a month, a certain part could vary in price by 30 percent. Standard cost takes an average of cost and applies it equally across the board. Activity-based costing, on the other hand, uses the price of each part by product line as well as any associated costs or savings. The same is true for labor, overhead, machinery, and anything else that impacts cost.

8   *Securities and Exchange Commission v. System Software Associates, Inc., Roger Covey and Joseph Skadra*, Civ. No. 00C 4240 (N.D. Ill.); http://www.sec.gov/litigation/litreleases/lr17770.htm.

9   Oracle (Redwood Shores, CA) and PeopleSoft (Pleasanton, CA) are two of the most dominant enterprise application players. Like SAP, they sell a complete set of business applications. Oracle, however, also sells a variety of pure technologies including databases, software development tools, and software infrastructure. Oracle and PeopleSoft had revenues of $9.6 billion and $1.9 billion, respectively, in 2002. At the end of 2003, Oracle was attempting to purchase PeopleSoft in a hostile takeover bid.

10 U.S. Department of Commerce, Bureau of Economic Analysis, "Private Fixed Investment in Equipment and Software by Type," National Income and Product Accounts Table 5.5; http:// www.bea.gov/bea/dn/nipaweb/SelectTable.asp?Selected=N. See also U.S. Department of Commerce, "Private Fixed Investment."

11 Corporate financial reports, company records and annual reports, and SEC filings.

12 U.S. Department of Commerce, Bureau of Economic Analysis, "Recognition of Business and Government Expenditures for Software as Investment: Methodology and Quantitative Impacts, 1958-98," by Robert Parker and Bruce Grimm, May 2000; http:// www.bea.gov/bea/about/software.pdf.

CHAPTER 3

1   Shelly Branch, "Hershey, Citing Technology Trouble, Says It Will Miss Earnings Estimates," *Wall Street Journal*, September 14, 1999, B12. This was the first of many stories about companies coming out of the closet with their technology implementation woes. Such stories did not focus on one vendor, but on many in proportion to their market penetration.

2   U.S. Department of Commerce, "Recognition of Business." Certain data was updated on September 3, 2002, and is available on the BEA web site. The data for the year 2002 is based on final software numbers published by the BEA and an estimation by the author.

3   A number of articles have told the history of FoxMeyer's woes. Two of the more comprehensive are M. L. Markus and R. I. Benjamin, "The Magic Bullet Theory in IT-Enabled Transformation," *Sloan Management Review* 38, no. 2 (Winter 1997): 55-68; http://www.mit-smr.com/past/1997/smr3824.html; and Dale Buss, "Nightmare," *Context Magazine*, Spring 1998; http://www.contextmag.com/setFrameRedirect.asp?src=/archives/199803/Feature3nightmare.asp.

4   A *chart of accounts* is a numbered listing of the titles of all accounts used in a company's bookkeeping system. They are listed first in the order they appear in the balance sheet and then in the order they appear in the income statement.

5   Erik Keller, "Enterprise Application Scenario" (presentation at the Gartner Fall Symposium, 1998).

6   U.S. Department of Commerce, "Recognition of Business."

CHAPTER 4

1   Alan Greenspan, Chairman, U.S. Federal Reserve Board, "The American Economy in a World Context" (remarks at the 35th Annual Conference on Bank Structure and Competition of the Federal Reserve Bank of Chicago, Chicago, IL, May 1999); http://www.federalreserve.gov/boarddocs/speeches/1999/19990506.htm.

2   Scott Adams, *Dilbert* cartoon strip, United Media, May 5, 1997.

3   *Customer relationship management* is a strategy that helps a company better understand the needs and aspects of all its customers. Software used to realize CRM consists of functionality that is used by sales, marketing, and service groups within a company. *Supply chain management* is a strategy that helps a company better control the creation and delivery of goods. Software that assists a company in this regard deals with the planning and execution of sourcing, production, and transportation of goods.

4   Robert Solow, "We'd Better Watch Out," review of *Manufacturing Matters: The Myth of the Post-Industrial Economy,* by Stephen S. Cohen and John Zysman, *New York Times*, July 12, 1987, 36.

5   McKinsey & Co., "U.S. Productivity Growth 1995-2000," MGI Report, October 2001; http://www.mckinsey.com/knowledge/mgi/productivity/.

6 Federal Reserve Board, "Information Technology and Productivity: Where Are We Now and Where Are We Going?" by Stephen Oliner and Daniel Sichel, May 2002; http://www.federalreserve.gov/pubs/feds/2002/200229/ 200229pap.pdf.

7 Harvard University and the Federal Reserve Board, "Raising the Speed Limit: U.S. Economic Growth in the Information Age," by Dale Jorgensen and Kevin Stiroh, May 2000; http://www.newyorkfed.org/research/economists/stiroh/ ks_grw.pdf.

8 National Bureau of Economic Research, "Does the 'New Economy' Measure Up to the Great Inventions of the Past?" NBER Working Paper 7833, by Robert Gordon, August 2000; http://papersdev.nber.org/papers/w7833.

9 Organisation for Economic Co-operation and Development, "Seizing the Benefits of ICT in a Digital Economy" (report from the meeting of the OECD Council, 2003); http://www1.oecd.org/ subject/mcm/2003/0003351E.pdf.

10 Strassmann Inc.; http://www.strassmann.com.

11 U.S. Department of Commerce, Economics and Statistics Administration, "Digital Economy 2002," February 2002; http:// www.esa.doc.gov/DigitalEconomy2002.cfm.

12 Gartner Inc. (http://www.gartner.com), META Group (http:// www.metagroup.com), Butler Group (http://www.butlergroup.com), and Datamonitor (http://www.datamonitor.com) have released reports over the last few years that are fairly consistent about the difficulty of success in CRM projects. All cite similar reasons (e.g., poor technology, cultural problems, project management) for failure.

13 Conference Board is a policy and research organization based in Washington, D.C. (http://www.conference-board.org). In 1997, KPMG-Canada (http://www.kpmg.ca/) surveyed 107 failed systems projects. The study "What Went Wrong? Unsuccessful Information Technology Projects" stated that lack of attention and financial goals were the chief reasons for failure. The study by Robins-Gioia LLC reflected these results, with a lower failure rate attributed to installations with good project-management backgrounds (http://www.robbinsgioia.com/news_events/ 012802_erp.aspx).

14 Bear, Stearns & Co.; http://www.bearstearns.com/bscportal/html/
    research/supplychain.htm. Nucleus Research;
    http://www.nucleusresearch.com/research/d1.pdf.

15 The Standish Group, "The CHAOS Report (1994)";
    http://www.standishgroup.com/sample_research/chaos_
    1994_1.php.

CHAPTER 5

1   Stephen Roach, "Capital Spending Myths," Morgan Stanley, March
    5, 2003; http://www.morganstanley.com/GEFdata/digests/
    20030305-wed.html. It should be noted that Mr. Roach is one of
    the few IT and economic growth curmudgeons in the financial
    research sector. His analysis, however, has been highly accurate over
    the past five years. He took a lot of heat in the late 1990s for his
    views, which are now common knowledge and accepted wisdom.
    "Irrational exuberance" is not in his lexicon.

2   Boston Consulting Group, "Tightening the Reigns on IT Spend-
    ing," by Wolfgang Thiel, Juliane Kronen, and Michael Grebe,
    November 2001; http://www.bcg.com/publications/
    publication_view.jsp?pubID=685&language=English.

3   McKinsey & Co., "Productivity Growth and Information Technol-
    ogy," MGI High Tech Practice, October 16, 2001. Thomas Pisello,
    *IT Value Chain Management, Maximizing the ROI from IT Invest-
    ments* (New Canaan, CT: Information Economics Press, 2003);
    http://www.infoeconomics.com/digital/show-ebook.php?id=10.

4   Bureau of Labor, Bureau of Economic Analysis data, and author
    estimates for 2003 expenditures.

5   In the spring of 2002, many stories were written on this topic.
    ZDNet put together one of the more comprehensive collections at
    http://zdnet.com.com/2251-1110-903233.html.

6   California State Auditor, Bureau of State Audits, "Enterprise
    Licensing Agreement: The State Failed to Exercise Due Diligence
    When Contracting with Oracle, Potentially Costing Taxpayers
    Millions of Dollars," April 2002; http://www.bsa.ca.gov/bsa/
    summaries/2001-128.html.

7   Peter Krass, "Software: A Terrible Thing to Waste," *CFO*, October
    2002; http://www.cfo.com/article/1,5309,7879||M|406,00.html.
    CFO magazine and Morgan Stanley conducted a software survey of
    more than 300 customers to look at usage and buying patterns.

8   Gartner, Inc., "Gartner Survey Shows 42 Percent of Purchased
    CRM Software Goes Unused," March 6, 2003;

http://www4.gartner.com/5_about/press_releases/
pr6mar2003a.jsp.

9 AMR Research, "The Overselling of Supply Chain Planning Suites: 60 Manufacturers Speak Up," August 2001; and "SCP: Better than You Have Been Led to Believe," by Larry Lapide, David O'Brien, and Wendy Davis, April 2003.

10 This survey was taken by the Sand Hill Group at its Enterprise 2003 conference in Liguna Niguel, CA, in June 2003. More than 150 executives of the software industry representing the entire range of sellers attended the conference.

11 U.S. Department of Energy; http://www.doe.gov.

12 Patricia Adams, "IT Asset Management Stages: Stairway to Heaven" (presentation at the Gartner Spring Symposium, 2003). Gartner has listed five levels of maturity for asset management. Level 1 is chaotic, which by definition states that little if anything is done to control assets. Level 2 is reactive and facilitates limited accountability by IT to manage assets. The proactive midpoint, Level 3, looks at an entire lifecycle to manage all costs from initial purchase to disposal. Levels 4 and 5 (service-oriented and value creation, respectively) deal with much higher levels of asset optimization and opportunity management.

CHAPTER 6

1 Andrew Grove, *Only the Paranoid Survive: How to Exploit the Crisis Points that Challenge Every Company and Career* (New York: Doubleday, 1996), 165. This quote by Grove is about the Internet. It applies equally well to the technologies and approaches discussed in this chapter.

2 Thomas Fuller, "How Microsoft Warded Off Rival Software," *New York Times,* May 15, 2003, Business Day, C1.

3 IBM believes that a significant amount of old software old continues to run the vast majority of the world's business processes. See "Enterprise Modernization: Leveraging Legacy Systems into Dynamic E-Business"; http://www-900.ibm.com/cn/software/websphere/products/download/whitepapers/G325-5410-00.pdf.

4 Saugatuck Technology and CFO Publishing are research partners. The two companies conducted joint research in the fall of 2002 concerning the technology spending priorities of CIOs and CFOs in the coming year.

5 Many standards fall under the moniker of web services, but four are the core: XML (Extensible Markup Language), SOAP (Simple

Object Access Protocol), UDDI (Universal Description, Discovery and Integration), and WSDL (Web Services Definition Language). XML is the protocol that is used to mark up and describe data; the other three specifications rely on this language. You can think of it as a common alphabet combined with a narrowly focused definition. SOAP is a technology that uses XML and assists in transferring data between two systems. It defines the format of a message. WSDL describes and links application functions over the Web. It is used to help construct applications that use multiple pieces of code or *services*. UDDI is used to define directories that exist on the Web; it permits the quick discovery of an address when queried.

6   Sand Hill Group, "Winning Strategies for Enterprise Software Vendors," July 2002. A companion report written for buyers of technology was released later that year. The authors of the report interviewed 117 executives at 76 companies who represented a cross-section of buyers and sellers interested in web services.

7   Sand Hill Group, "Enterprises Race for Competitive Leadership," January 2003. This study lists 60 case studies of companies that have built pilots and operational systems using web-services technologies.

8   Ken Berryman and Greg Hughes (McKinsey & Co.), "The Maturation of the Enterprise Software Industry" (slide taken from a presentation at Enterprise 2003, June 2003).

9   It is difficult to make blanket statements about how appropriate different technologies are for different types of tasks. A small computing load would be the running of a business application and systems for a small division of a major corporation with hundreds of users—for example, a financial or inventory system for a services center or a manufacturing plant. A medium computing load would involve the running of multiple business applications and systems linking multiple sites of a major corporation—for example, order processing and inventory check and allotment for a multinational corporation. A large computing load represents the most complex and transaction-intensive types of applications. Such a load would include running stock exchanges, taking airline reservations, and processing financial transactions worldwide.

These statements only indicate an order of magnitude; they cannot account for all the diversity in computing use. For instance, the online trading company eBay has very large computing requirements. According to its annual report, in 2002 it had a peak usage of 580 million page views per day, 60 million item searches per day, and 4.5 gigabits per second of data traffic. It uses a combination of

Sun Microsystems Solaris, Microsoft NT, and Linux operating systems and hardware to run its trading network. These computing systems are not typically associated with large computing requirements, yet they work well for eBay.

10 Tom Bittman, "The Future of Windows in the Data Center" (presentation at the Gartner Spring Symposium, 2003). OLTP (online transaction processing) is the way in which many commercial applications are executed. The ability of a computing system to handle different OLTP loads (both speed and number of transactions) is an indication of the size of computing resources needed. Microsoft Datacenter is a high-end version of Microsoft's operating systems that is used by companies with large computing requirements.

11 Morgan Stanley CIO Survey Series, Release 4.0 (May 2003).

12 George Weiss, "The Future of Linux in the Enterprise" (presentation at the Gartner Spring Symposium, 2003), 4. META Group has made similar predictions concerning the growth of Linux; http://www.cnn.com/2002/TECH/biztech/12/10/meta.linux.reut/.

13 Robert A. Guth, "Google: Free to Choose, Linux May Be the Biggest Threat Microsoft Faces. Even Microsoft, at Last, Seems to Recognize That," *Wall Street Journal*, May 19, 2003, R6.

14 The Apache Software Foundation (http://www.apache.org) is a not-for-profit organization that facilitates widespread programmer and user collaboration to promote and spread open-source software projects. Although it supports and is working on over a dozen projects, it is best known for its Apache HTTP web server technology.

15 Fuller, "How Microsoft Warded Off Rival Software."

CHAPTER 7

1 This comment comes from Ed Yourdon's web site (http://www.yourdon.com), where he writes on topics of general interest to technologists.

2 Sykes Enterprises Inc., Form 10-K filing, 2003; http://www.sec.gov/Archives/edgar/data/1010612/000095014403003631/g81313e10vk.htm. This document states that Sykes handles 600,000 calls per day from 40 call centers around the world; 15 are in the United States, 3 are in Canada, 15 are in Europe, and 7 are elsewhere in the world. In the United States, the average call center has 432 seats that handle 12,000 calls per day; this implies that there are 6,500 seats in the United States.

In reporting its third-quarter 2003 financial results, Sykes said it planned to have between 9,600 and 11,000 offshore seats by the middle of 2004.

3 Marianne Kolbasuk McGee, "Sliver of the Pie," *InformationWeek*, April 28, 2003; http://www.informationweek.com/story/showArticle.jhtml?articleID=9300001.

4 American Electronics Association, "High-Tech Workforce Shrinks by 560,000 Jobs Over Two Years"; http://www.aeanet.org/pressroom/idmk_2002_tech_employment_press.asp.

The Information Technology Association of America is a trade association based in Arlington, VA, representing the information technology industry. It tracks industry and employment trends that are important to buyers and sellers of IT. Its most recent employment survey, "2003 IT Workplace Survey," was presented at the National IT National Workforce Convocation (May 5, 2003). Definitions of job categories can be found at http://www.itaa.org.

5 The U.S. Bureau of Labor tracks U.S. employment and productivity statistics; see http://www.bls.gov/oes/2000/oes_15Co.htm and http://www.bls.gov/oes/2001/oes150000.htm.

6 Paul Roberts, "Harvard Event Showcases Russia as Outsourcing Site," *Computerworld*, May 1, 2003; http://ww.computerworld.com/careertopics/careers/story/0,10801,80852,00.html.

7 "Ask the Source," *CIO* Magazine. *CIO* sets up an interactive web site where industry experts post answers to questions posed. This quotation appears in a dialogue that occurred between June 1 and June 17, 2003; http://www2.cio.com/ask/source/2003/questions/question1668.html.

8 Joanna Slater, "GE Takes Advantage of India's Talented Research Pool," *Wall Street Journal*, March 26, 2003.

9 PeopleSoft, "PeopleSoft Expands Operations in India," May 6, 2003; http://www.peoplesoft.com/corp/en/about/press/press_release.jsp?doc=32F55EF9C94E63D688256D1E00580DAA.

10 Oracle; http://www.oracle.com/broadband/showondemand.html?1421243.

11 Forrester Research, "3.3 million U.S. Services Jobs to Go Offshore," by John McCarthy, November 11, 2002.

12 NASSCOM, "Strategic Review 2003: Revisiting the Forecasts," February 21, 2003; http://www.nasscom.org/artdisplay.asp?Art_id=1614.

13 NASSCOM; http://www.nasscom.org.

14 Chinese Software Industry Association; http://www.csia.org.cn/ chinese_en/.

15 National Science Foundation, Division of Science Resources Statistics, "Science and Engineering Degrees, 1966–2000"; http:// www.nsf.gov/sbe/srs/nsf02327/pdfstart.htm and http:// www.nsf.gov/sbe/srs/seind02/pdf/c02.pdf.

16 Stephen Roach, "The World's Only Growth Story," Morgan Stanley, November 4, 2002; http://www.morganstanley.com/GEFdata/ digests/20021104-mon.html#anchor0.

17 World Bank Group, "China Data Profile," World Development Indicators database, April 2003; http://devdata.worldbank.org/ external/CPProfile.asp?SelectedCountry=CHN&CCODE= CHN&CNAME=China&PTYPE=CP.

18 Development Research Centre, "The Government and Guanxi: The Chinese Software Industry in Transition," DRC Working Paper 19, by Anne Lee Saxenian, University of California at Berkeley, March 2003, 32; http://www.london.edu/cnem/ Current_Research/Development_Centre/DRC_Working_Papers/ DRC19.pdf.

19 V. P. Kharbanda and Yogesh Suman, "Chinese Initiative in the Software Industry: Quest to Leap," *Current Science* 83, no.12 (December 25, 2002); http://www.ias.ac.in/currsci/dec252002/1450.pdf.

20 NASSCOM, "India and China Herald a New Era of IT Cooperation," June 26, 2003; http://www.nasscom.org/artdisplay.asp ?Art_id=1881.

21 SEI-CMM stands for the Software Engineering Institute-Capability Model. This model is managed by SEI, which is sponsored by the U.S. Department of Defense and Carnegie Mellon University. It is a five-level methodology to assess and improve software processes by modeling, defining, and measuring the maturity of those processes. Its levels are initial, repeatable, defined, managed, and optimized. Companies that are certified for Level 4 or 5 are considered to have the highest quality for software development, much like the six-sigma certification for defects in manufacturing that was promoted by General Electric and Motorola.

22 SEI, "Compiled List of Organizations Who Have Publicly Announced Their Maturity Levels After Having an Appraisal Performed," April 17, 2003; http://seir.sei.cmu.edu/pml/.

23 U.S. Department of Labor, Bureau of Labor Statistics, "Industries with the Fastest Wage and Salary Employment Growth, 2000-2010"; http://www.bls.gov/news.release/ecopro.t03.htm.

24 U.S. Department of Labor, Bureau of Labor Statistics, "Occupations with the Largest Job Growth, 2000-10"; http://www.bls.gov/news.release/ecopro.t07.htm.

CHAPTER 8

1 Mylene Mangalindan, "Larry Ellison's Sober Vision," *Wall Street Journal*, April 8, 2003.

2 The World Information Technology and Services Alliance (WITSA), *Digital Planet 2002: The Global Information Economy* (Arlington, VA: February 2002); http://www.itaa.org/news/pubs/product.cfm?EventID=172. The data for this study was contributed by International Data Corp. IDC said that hardware spending would drop by 0.5 percent in 2003: "Continued Economic and Geopolitical Uncertainties Lead IDC to Revise Outlook for Worldwide IT Spending in 2003," April 3, 2003; http://www.idc.com/getdoc.jhtml;jsessionid=UYXBW4BDJ3O0SCT FA4FSFFAKMUDYUIWD?containerId=pr2003_04_02_123536.

3 Sarbanes-Oxley was a bill passed by the U.S. Congress in 2002 in response to the shenanigans of corporations, CEOs, auditors, and others in charge of financial oversight and reporting. It requires much more disclosure and transparency of the financial workings of publicly held companies. If companies do not follow the rules set forth by Sarbanes-Oxley and are not compliant with its specifications for disclosure, the executives and board of directors can be held personally liable and can be fined, sent to jail, or both.

4 Eric Chabrow, "IT Staffs Lack Financial Chops for Project Analysis," *InformationWeek*, March 24, 2003; http://www.informationweek.com/story/showArticle.jhtml?articleID=8700123. This story details a study by Northwest University and Diamond Cluster International that surveyed CIOs or CTOs in large companies. It states that little if any financial analysis takes place when IT decisions are made. Another report by Ernst & Young LLP that was released in the summer of 2002 echoes those results.

5 U.S. General Accounting Office, "Business Systems Modernization: Summary of GAO's Assessment of the Department of Defense's Initial Business Enterprise Architecture," July 7, 2003; http://www.gao.gov/new.items/d03877r.pdf.

6 William Bulkeley, "For Clues Why Tech Is Still Down, See Mr. Kheradpir," *Wall Street Journal*, March 11, 2003.

7 Sand Hill Group, Enterprise 2003.

8 WITSA, *Digital Planet 2002.* IDC said that worldwide IT spending would increase by only 1 percent in 2003: "Global IT Spending Remains Flat Amidst Tentative Signs of U.S. Economic Recovery, According to IDC," July 16, 2003; http://www.idc.com/ getdoc.jhtml;jsessionid=TLEEUWJEGQB4OCTFA4FCFFAK MUDYWIWD?containerId=pr2003_07_15_150906.

CHAPTER 9

1 Society for the Promotion of Buddhism, *The Teaching of Buddha* (Tokyo: 1966), 76, 78.

2 WITSA, *Digital Planet 2002.*

3 *Jennifer Mears and Phil Hochmuth*, "Server Consolidation Helps Jet-Blue Soar," *Network World*, June 9, 2003; http://www.nwfusion.com/news/2003/0609jetblue.html.

CHAPTER 10

1 U.S. Department of Labor, Bureau of Labor Statistics; http://www.bls.gov.

2 C.P. Snow, *The Two Cultures* (Cambridge: Cambridge University Press, 1993).

CHAPTER 11

1 Red Herring, "Ray Lane Paved Oracle's Path," October 1, 2000; http://www.redherring.com/Article.aspx?f=articles/archive/mag/ issue83/mag-profile-83.xml. Ray Lane, former president and COO, explained how Oracle obtained $1 billion in operational savings. This article states, "[Lane] challenges [the] well-publicized claim that the company trimmed $1 billion in operating costs by using Oracle software throughout the company. Mr. Lane explains that this was absolutely not the case. 'The billion dollars in savings has come from control of expenses,' he says. 'Specifically, we grew the sales force at 5 to 7 percent in the last few years, while sales grew at 15 percent.'"

2 IBM, "LEGO Company Builds for the Future with IBM"; http://www.ibm.com/news/us/2003/08/111.html.

3 An earlier version of this chart was created by the author when he was an analyst at Gartner and was part of the 1998 Gartner Fall Symposium presentation "Enterprise Application Scenario."

4   Saugatuck Technology Inc., "Utility Computing: A Hard Sell" (July 2003); http://www.saugatech.com/stucorder.htm.

EPILOGUE

1   Lewis Mumford, *Technics and Civilization* (New York: Harcourt, Brace and Co., 1934), 434.

2   Sean Young, "Intel CEO Won't Predict IT Recovery Yet," *Information Week*, August 26, 2003; http://www.informationweek.com/story/showArticle.jhtml?articleID=13900125.

3   RFID (radio-frequency identification) is a technology that uses inexpensive semiconductor chips placed on products and assets so they can be tracked and located. It has great potential to help companies manage product and supply chain costs. Within the next three to five years, the cost per RFID tag is expected to hit 5 cents or less when the tags are purchased in volume. Wireless technologies represent a collection of different hardware and software that provides a wide degree of mobility for computing devices. Voice Over IP is a technology that transmits voice communications over the same lines used to transmit Internet data.

PERMISSIONS

Copyrighted materials have been reprinted with permission from AMR Research Inc., BDNA, Gartner Inc., McKinsey and Company, McKinsey Global Institute, NASSCOM, National Snow and Ice Center at the University of Colorado, Saugatuck Technology and CFO Publishing, Scott Polar Research Institute at the University of Cambridge, and Strassmann Inc.

index